Shared Water Resources in West Africa

International Water Law

Volumes published in this Brill Research Perspectives title are listed at *brill.com/rpwl*

Shared Water Resources in West Africa

Relevance and Application of the UN Watercourses and the UNECE Water Conventions

By

Nwamaka Chigozie Odili

BRILL

LEIDEN | BOSTON

This paperback book edition is simultaneously published as issue 3.1 (2018) of *International Water Law*
DOI 10.1163/23529369-12340009.

Library of Congress Control Number: 2017964105

Typeface for the Latin, Greek, and Cyrillic scripts: "Brill". See and download: brill.com/brill-typeface.

ISBN 978-90-04-36482-0 (paperback)
ISBN 978-90-04-36483-7 (e-book)

This book is printed on acid-free paper and produced in a sustainable manner.

Contents

List of Figures and Tables

Figures

Table

Shared Water Resources in West Africa

Relevance and Application of the UN Watercourses and the UNECE Water Conventions

Nwamaka Chigozie Odili
Legal Officer, Federal Ministry of Justice, Abuja, Nigeria
amaka142@yahoo.com

Abstract

Since the adoption of the General Act of Berlin in 1885, which dealt, *inter alia*, with the Niger River, more agreements have been contracted for the management of some of the shared watercourses in West Africa, particularly in the post-colonial era. Although only six out of its numerous shared watercourses are regulated by legal instruments, West Africa contributed through these agreements to the development of international water prior to the adoption of the UN Watercourses and the UNECE Water Conventions in the 1990s. Initial instruments dealt primarily with navigation, while later agreements addressed the need for co-operation and incorporated other principles of customary international water law. The two conventions have, no doubt, influenced this trend, raising the question of whether riparian states in West Africa need to be parties to either or both water conventions to enhance management, sharing, and protections of their shared watercourses.

Keywords

navigation – shared watercourses – UN Watercourses Convention – UNECE Water Convention – West Africa

Introduction

Treaty development and practice for managing transboundary water resources in West Africa have been gradual, evolving from the pre-colonial era through the post-colonial era to the present. Within the colonial period, not much was achieved on shared watercourses' agreement in West Africa. The first attempt to manage shared watercourses in West Africa was the 1884 General Act of

 | DOI 10.1163/9789004364837_002

Berlin, which evolved from the Berlin West African Conference.[1] According to Salman, the General Act of Berlin was an extension of the principle of the Vienna Congress of 1815 for uses of shared rivers in Europe which established "freedom of navigation for all the riparian states on the shared river."[2] The instrument was only applicable to the Congo River in Central Africa and Niger River in West Africa. At this time "the principle of freedom of navigation was of a paramount importance to the European powers in their colonial expansion and the development of their colonial activities."[3] Hence, the great rivers of Africa offered the colonial powers highway access into the African continent. Chapter V of the General Act of Berlin, titled Act of Navigation on the Niger was meant to allow easy access to the colonists into West Africa through the Niger River.

By 1919 World War I had ended and most colonists had settled in their colonies. Hence there was need to revise the General Act of Berlin, and the Convention on Revision of General Act of Berlin and General Acts and Declaration of Brussels (the 1919 Convention) was adopted to replace it.[4] The 1919 Convention adopted almost all the provisions of the General Act of Berlin but also further opened the Niger River to all contracting parties and members of the League of Nations.[5] Within this colonial period, specific basin agreements were rare in West Africa but in 1935 Mauritania and Senegal established the *Organisation Autonome dela Vallée* (OAV) and the Senegal River Basin Development Mission or *Mission d'Aménagement du Bassin du Fleuve Sénégal*

1 The General Act of Berlin was adopted at Berlin on 26th day of February, 1885, http://waado.org/colonial_rule/general_documents/berlin_act_1885.html. The Berlin West African Conference (15 November 1884 to 26 February 1885) was a series of meetings at which major European powers negotiated and formalized claims to territory in Africa, a process known as the 'Scramble for Africa'. See Oxford Reference Encyclopaedia of Africa. http://www.oxfordreference.com/view/10.1093/acref/9780195337709.001.0001/acref-9780195337709-e-0467 (accessed 30 November 2016).

2 M. A. Salman 'River Niger', *Max Planck Encyclopedia of Public International Law* http://opil.ouplaw.com/view/10.1093/law:epil/9780199231690/law-9780199231690-e1325?prd=EPIL (accessed 26 July 2017).

3 Laurence Boisson de Chazournes, 'Freshwater and International Law: the Interplay between Universal, Regional and Basin Perspectives' (Paris, UNESCO, 2009). http://archive-ouverte.unige.ch:5080 (accessed 30 January 2017).

4 Adopted at Saint-Germain-en-Laye, 10 September 1919 after the First World War (the 1919 Convention). https://www.loc.gov/law/help/us-treaties/bevans/m-ust000002-0261.pdf (accessed 30 November 2016).

5 1919 Convention on Revision of the General Act of Berlin, arts. 5 and 6.

(MAS) for cooperation at the Senegal River Basin.[6] Further, there is record of border sharing agreements between French and Great Britain concerning the Volta River Basin.[7]

By the 1960s many West African nations had become independent and so the need arose to cooperate and manage the shared water resources in a way that suits the riparian states. The post-colonial era is therefore characterized by the first indigenous instruments for regulating use of different transboundary watercourses in West Africa. The first such instrument is the Convention Relating to the General Development of the Senegal River (the Bamako Convention)[8] which was followed by the Act Regarding Navigation and Economic Co-operation between the States of the Niger Basin (the Act of Niamey). The Act of Niamey abrogated relevance of both the 1885 General Act of Berlin and the 1919 treaty to the Niger River Basin.[9] The Niger River Commission was subsequently established by the 1964 Niger River Commission Agreement.[10] On May 22, 1964 the Lake Chad Basin Convention was also adopted. By the 1970s and 1980s more instruments were contracted for the Niger, Senegal, Gambia, and Koliba-Korubal River basins. Since then many transboundary water agreements and treaties have been adopted in West Africa.

---

6 See Makane Mbengue 'A Model for African Shared Water Resources: The Senegal River Legal System,' *Review of European Community and International Environmental Law*, Vol. 23 No. 1 (2014), pp. 59–66.

7 The agreements are the Exchange of Notes between France and Great Britain relative to the Boundary between the Gold Coast and French Soudan and the Agreement between France and Great Britain relative to the frontier between French and British possessions from the Gulf of Guinea to the Niger (Southern Nigeria and Dahomey) which affected the Volta River Basin.

8 Convention Relating to the General Development of the Senegal River, Bamako, 26 July 1963 https://iea.uoregon.edu/treaty-text/1963-bamakosenegalriverbasinfrtxt (accessed 31 January 2017).

9 Act Regarding Navigation and Economic Co-operation between the States of the Niger Basin, Niamey, 26 October 1963, http://gis.nacse.org/tfdd/tfdddocs/264ENG.pdf. (accessed 1 December 2016). Article 1 of the Act of Niamey states that the General Act of Berlin of 26 February 1885, the General Act and Declaration of Brussels of 2 July, 1890, and the Convention of Saint-Germain-en-Laye, 10th September, 1919 are and remain abrogated as far as they concern the Niger River, its tributaries, and sub-tributaries.

10 Agreement Concerning the River Niger Commission and the Navigation and Transport on the River Niger, Niamey, 25 November 1964 http://iea.uoregon.edu/treaty-text/1964-nigerrivercommissionnavigationtransportrivernigerentxt. (accessed 1 December 2016).

The implication of these initiatives is that riparian states in West Africa had achieved collaboration and joint management of some of its shared watercourses long before the adoption of the Convention on the Law of Non-navigational Uses of International Watercourses (UN Watercourses Convention)[11] and the Convention on the Protection and the Use of Transboundary Watercourses and International Lakes (UNECE Water Convention).[12] However, considering the whole region, the need to manage transboundary watercourses in an equitable and sustainable manner has not been given prime recognition at the political level and so has not advanced significantly. Although the region has twenty-five shared watercourses, only six have some sort of cooperative arrangements in place.[13] Most of the region's numerous shared watercourses agreements and treaties concentrate on a few transboundary watercourses resulting in a scenario of too many instruments for a few shared watercourses and little or nothing for others. The majority of the regimes are flawed with failing and gaps. Despite the need for improvement, West Africa has recorded some success stories and other regions could learn from its progress in transboundary water management.[14]

The water regimes from the West African region are recognized among numerous instruments for regulating shared watercourses around the world.[15] However, of all these water regimes the UN Watercourses Convention and the UNECE Water Convention stand out as the two principle UN water treaties for

11 The UN Watercourses Convention was adopted by the General Assembly of United Nations in New York on 21 May 1997. Available online at http://legal.un.org/ilc/texts/instruments/english/conventions/8_3_1997.pdf (accessed 22 February 2015).

12 The Economic Commission for Europe (UNECE) is one of the six UN Regional Commissions. The UNECE Water Convention was adopted and signed in Helsinki on 17 March 1992. Available online at http://www.unece.org/fileadmin/DAM/env/water/pdf/watercon.pdf (accessed 22 February 2015).

13 'Atlas on Regional Integration in West Africa: Transboundary River Basins'. ECOWAS-SWAC and Organisation for Economic Cooperation and Development (2006) http://www.oecd.org/swac/publications/38409569.pdf. (accessed 15 January 2015).

14 According to Mbengue (n 6), the Senegal River Basin regime follows the advanced concept of integrated river basin development and has not only fostered cooperation over the management of the river basin but "has influenced the development of the law of international watercourse in Africa."

15 According to the Food and Agricultural Organization of the United Nations (FAO), more than 3,600 treaties related to international water resources were drawn up between 805 and 1984 AD, while a further 400 water agreements were signed since 1820. See United Nations Environment Programme (UNEP) "Atlas of International Freshwater Agreements (Nairobi, UNEP, 2002) at 6, http://www.unep.org/publications/search/pub_details_s.asp?ID=115 (accessed 30 March 2015).

the managing shared watercourses.[16] Although the provisions of both instruments are not conflicting, there are challenges in having two 'global' treaties on the same subject matter. The practicability of enforcing the provisions of the treaties for transboundary water resources management at the same time in the same region, such as West Africa must be considered. As a result of activities of the UN Watercourses Convention Global Initiative,[17] some countries in West Africa embraced the call for ratification of the UN Watercourses Convention and became parties to the Convention.[18] The concept of 'universalisation' of the UNECE Water Convention came up more recently as a result of the long delay in the entry into force of the UN Watercourses Convention which, although adopted in 1997, only entered into force in 2014. At the regional level, the UNECE Water Convention has been in force since 1996, and with its current globalization efforts extend its activities beyond Europe to parts of Africa including West Africa.[19] Articles 25 and 26 of the Convention were amended to allow non-UNECE states who are members of the United Nations to become contracting parties to the Convention. "The amendment entered into force on 6 February 2013, turning the Water Convention into a

16 For 20 years the UNECE Water Convention proved to be an effective regional instrument for managing transboundary water resources in Europe but, as discussed below, has been opened to all UN member states.

17 The UN Watercourses Convention Global Initiative was launched by the Worldwide Fund for Nature (WWF) in 2006 to promote and accelerate the ratification process of the UN Watercourses Convention. The members of this Initiative are the WWF; Green Cross; UNESCO Centre for Water Law; Policy and Science; University of Dundee; UN Secretary-General's Advisory Board on Water and Sanitation; Global Nature Fund; Global Water Partnership and International Union for Conservation of Nature. See Alistair Rieu-Clarke et al. (eds) *UN Watercourses Convention (Users' Guide)* (IHP-HELP, Centre for Water Law, Policy and Science), University of Dundee, 2012) at 23.

18 In West Africa, Nigeria, Benin, Guinea Bissau and Burkina Faso are contracting parties to the UN Watercourses Convention.

19 At the 6th Meeting of the Parties in 2012, non-UNECE parties including the Democratic Republic of Congo, Namibia, and the South African Development Community (SADC) Secretariat participated. See Nataliya Nikiforova, 'International Conventions on Transboundary Waters: Global Solution to Regional Challenges.' Presentation at the 1st International Conference on Energy and Water, Luanda, 25–27 September 2013. http://www.aceew.org/apresentacoes/26/7.pdf?PHPSESSID=62uihl96ajftdm57plkd5q07e2 (accessed 5 January 2015). The Niger River Basin in West Africa and the North West Sahara Aquifer in North Africa have been nominated for study under the UNECE Water Convention, water-food-energy-ecosystems nexus project.

legal framework for transboundary water cooperation worldwide."[20] While no country in West Africa is a contracting party to the UNECE Water Convention, this could change in the near future.

Given these current developments in international water law and the current status of transboundary water cooperation in West Africa, this research considers whether accession to both UN water treaties can strengthen cooperation in the region by providing regulatory framework for basins without instruments and filling in the gaps in existing water regimes. A key question to be addressed is whether the provisions of the UNECE Water Convention offer any additional benefits to West African states over and above the UN Watercourses Convention. Should countries who are contracting parties to the UN Watercourses Convention also become parties to the UNECE Water Convention? What is the best option available for shared watercourses governance in West Africa?

In order to address these key research questions this monograph will first examine the transboundary water systems in West Africa and its treaty evolution and practices for management of shared watercourses prior to the adoption of the UN water treaties. This discussion will highlight the success stories in the region regarding share watercourses' management during this period. The second section comprises a comparative analysis of both UN water treaties, including areas of similarities and differences, to determine their relevance as global instruments for management of transboundary water resources. Following this examination, section three will present an in-depth analysis of the current treaty landscape of transboundary water management in West Africa vis-à-vis the UN water treaties. This will expose the strengths and weaknesses of specific treaty regimes in West Africa, their peculiar features, and the influence of the global treaties. This section will pose and answer the question of which UN water treaty is more beneficial to West Africa. The fourth section provides an overview of activities under the UNECE Water Convention and deals with the question of whether this convention is a 'legitimate' treaty for West Africa. Finally, this monograph will resolve the question of what is the best position to be adopted in the context of transboundary water resources management in West Africa.

20 'Introduction: About the UNECE Water Convention,' *UNECE* http://www.unece.org/env/water/text/text.html. (accessed 24 July 2017).

1.0 Transboundary Water Systems in West Africa

1.1 *Key Challenges for Cooperation over Transboundary Waters in West Africa*

West Africa is made up of 16 countries and 25 international watercourses (Figure 1).[21] With the exception of Cape Verde, all the other countries in the region share at least one transboundary watercourse[22] which represents potential cooperation requirements in a little less than half of the 59 transboundary fresh water basins available in Africa.[23] Of all the shared watercourses in West Africa, only six major shared watercourses have agreements to manage and regulate their uses (Table 1). Twenty shared watercourses in the region have no basin-specific instruments regulating the use of water resources and activities at the basin (Table 1).[24]

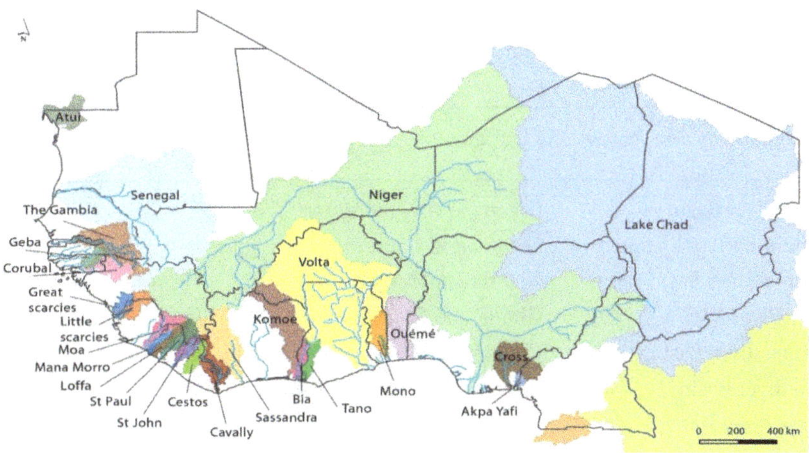

FIGURE 1 *Shared watercourses in West Africa.*
SOURCE: 'ATLAS OF REGIONAL INTEGRATION IN WEST AFRICA' (N13)

21 The countries of West Africa are Burkina Faso, Benin, Côte d'Ivoire, Ghana, The Gambia, Guinea, Guinea-Bissau, Liberia, Mali, Mauritania, Niger, Nigeria, Senegal, Sierra Leone, Togo and Cape Verde. According to OECD, there are 28 transboundary river basins in West Africa but only 25 are identified in the figure above (See Atlas of Regional Integration, n 13 at 3).

22 Ibid., (n 13) at 4.

23 UNEP (n 15) at 1.

24 'The United Nations Convention on the Law of the Non-Navigational Uses of International Watercourses and West Africa's Transboundary Water System'. (Publication sponsored by ECOWAS, GWP, Green Cross, International Water Association, WWF and UNESCO Centre for Water Law, Policy and Science, April 2011) at 4.

TABLE 1 *Transboundary watercourses in West Africa.*

Regulated

Transboundary watercourse	Riparian states
Niger River Basin	Nigeria, Niger, Burkina Faso, Côte d'Ivoire, Benin, Cameroun, Guinea, Mali, Chad
Lake Chad Basin	Cameroun, Nigeria, Chad, Central African Republic, Niger, Libya
Volta River Basin	Ghana, Burkina Faso, Benin, Togo, Côte d'Ivoire and Mali
Senegal River Basin	Senegal, Guinea, Mali, Mauritania
Gambia River Basin	Gambia, Guinea, Guinea Bissau, Senegal
Koliba-Korubal River Basin	Guinea and Guinea Bissau

Non-Regulated

Transboundary watercourse	Riparian states
Cross River Basin	Nigeria and Cameroon
Akpa Yafi River Basin	Nigeria and Cameroon
Queme River Basin	Nigeria and Benin
Tano River Basin	Ghana and Côte d'Ivoire
Komoe River Basin	Côte d'Ivoire, Ghana and Burkina Faso
Atui River Basin	Mauritania and West Sahara
Mono River Basin	Togo and Benin
Bia River Basin	Ghana and Côte d'Ivoire
Sassandra River Basin	Guinea and Côte d'Ivoire
Cavally River Basin	Côte d'Ivoire, Guinea and Liberia
Cestos River Basin	Côte d'Ivoire, Guinea and Liberia
St John River Basin	Liberia and Guinea
St. Paul River Basin	Liberia and Guinea
Loffa River Basin	Liberia and Guinea
Mana Morro River Basin	Liberia and Sierra Leone
Moa River Basin	Liberia, Sierra Leone and Guinea
Little Scarcies River Basin	Sierra Leone and Guinea
Great Scarcies River Basin	Sierra Leone and Guinea
Geba River Basin	Guinea Bissau, Guinea and Senegal

SOURCE: AUTHOR

Although only few transboundary watercourses in West Africa are covered by specific agreements, countries are strongly interdependent as regards water resources. Some major rivers in the region such as the Niger, Senegal and Gambia Rivers, rise in areas with a lot of rainfall before crossing the Sahelian zones with their chronic rainfall deficits, and finally descending into areas with high rainfall before emptying into the Atlantic Ocean. Accordingly, this condition allows "fresh water transfer from wetlands to arid areas and creates a strong interdependence of the countries with regard to use of fresh water resources."[25] Similarly, the region's only transboundary lake, Lake Chad, is also situated in the Sahel region where there is minimal rainfall. These two conditions, coupled with the impacts of climate change, urbanization, and overpopulation, lead to an abundance of fresh water in some countries while others have limited or scarce availability of the resource.

Figure 2 represents an index of dependency of the total share of renewable water resources of a country in West Africa produced outside its borders. Niger and Mauritania have about 90% dependency. It has been observed that, in West Africa, pressure on water resources for the needs of agricultural growth, industrial and urban development will increase significantly in the next 20 years.[26] Hence there is urgent need for collaboration in managing water resources not only because of the region's interdependency on available fresh water but also because of other aggravating factors that put pressure on shared water resources. This pressure creates tension that could lead to full-fledged conflict.[27] On the contrary, shared water resources can be a catalyst and reason for cooperation and good neighborliness among countries if the resources are managed collaboratively. According to Vinogradov et al., conflicts in the utilization of water resources can arise between existing uses, between existing

25 See Economic Community of West African States (ECOWAS) West Africa Water Resources Policy, adopted 19 December 2008. http://cmsdata.iucn.org/downloads/wawrp.pdf. (accessed 17 September 2017)

26 Sylviane Tabarly, "La frontière, discontinuités et dynamiques: Bassins versants transfrontaliers en Afrique occidentale", *Geoconfluences, DGESCO—ENS de Lyon* (2008), 'http://geoconfluences.ens-lyon.fr/doc/typespace/frontier/FrontDoc.htm (accessed 30 August 2017).

27 Amidou Garane 'UN Watercourses Convention: Applicability and Relevance in West Africa' (Global Water Partnership, WWF, Green Cross and UNESCO Centre of Water Law, Policy and Science, 2008) http://internationalwaterlaw.org/bibliography/WWF/RA_West_Africa.pdf (accessed 26 January 2017). Examples include the Nigeria/Niger conflict concerning the Kandadji Dam project in Niger and the 1998 conflict between Senegal and Mauritania over fossil valleys rehabilitation project.

and new uses and over future uses.[28] Such conflicts could be transformed into cooperation through basin agreements and treaties that provide the means and processes of resolving the conflicts. Mostert also identifies three areas of water conflicts and suggests that these could become a "catalyst for regional peace and development through dialogue, co-operation, and participative management of the resource."[29]

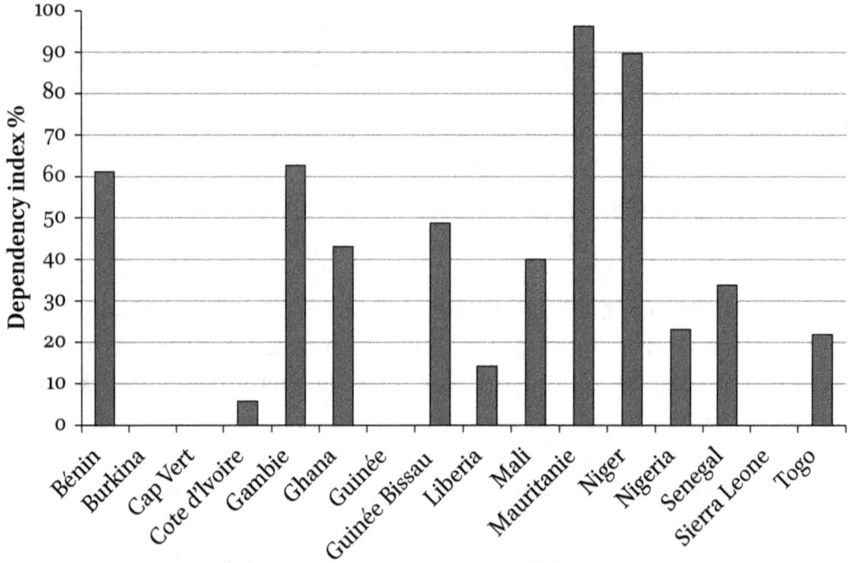

FIGURE 2 *Dependency (as %) of the total share of renewable water resources in West Africa by country.*
SOURCE: FAO-AQUASTAT (2005)[30]

---

28 S. Vinogradov et al., *Transforming Potential Conflict into Co-operation Potential. The Role of International Water Law.* PCCP Series No. 2 (Paris, UNESCO, 2003). According to Wouters, "where issues of legal entitlement of water resources arise, the determination of what is equitable and reasonable will be the basis of the overall solution." 'The Legal Response to International Water Scarcity and Water Conflicts: The UN Watercourses Convention and Beyond,' *The Water Page*, http://www.africanwater.org/pat_wouters1.htm (accessed 30 August 2017). See also H. L. Beach et al., *Transboundary Freshwater Dispute Resolution* (New York, United Nations University Press, 2000) who stress the need to include conflict resolution mechanisms in agreements before disputes arise.

29 Mostert identifies three areas of conflict: collective problems namely, issues in which all countries concerned have similar interests, such as the ecological restoration of an international lake or the joint development of a boundary river; negative externality problems, which are actual or proposed activities in one country that have negative effects on another country, such as upstream water diversions and water pollution; and positive

1.2 *Treaty Evolution and Development for Management of Shared Watercourses in West Africa*

Traditionally, in West Africa water is seen as gift from God and there is no conception of managing the resource. Also, before colonization and the formation of countries in West Africa, people lived in communities, not countries and society was less complex. With colonization countries emerged, as did urbanization, which had an impact on the environment and river basins. Hence the need emerged to manage all shared resources, including water resources. Although the principles of customary international law apply in all cases whether there are regulatory instruments or not, treaties are needed for strengthening the international water law system because they create obligations.[31] According to de Chazournes,

> the rule of law plays a significant role in managing transboundary freshwater resources ... Laws ... provide a means of finding potential solutions to international water problems. Co-operation on transboundary water resources is unlikely to be established sustainably without appropriate legal support.[32]

Leb further notes that riparian states on many international watercourses enhanced their cooperative relationship in managing, utilizing, protecting, and developing their shared watercourse through mutual agreements with international treaties that describe how the resources should be managed and provide specific rules of conduct.[33] According to Ayibotele, an understanding that a

externality problems, which includes activities in a country that would benefit another country, such as the construction of a dam that would reduce flooding downstream. Conflicts are most common due to collective problems. E. Mostert, *Conflict and Co-operation in the Management of International Freshwater Resources: A Global Review*, PCCP Series No. 19 (Paris, UNESCO, 2003). http://unesdoc.unesco.org/images/0013/001333/133305e.pdf (accessed 30 August 2017).

30 Information is obtained from ECOWAS, *Regional Water Policy* (Appendices) at 5. Available at ECOWAS Water Coordinate Centre Burkina Faso.

31 Treaties create binding obligations, which is different from the weaker norms of customary international law.

32 Boisson de Chazournes, (n 3) at 1.

33 Chrisrina Leb, *Co-operation in the Law of Transboundary Water Resources.* (New York, Cambridge University Press, 2013) at 2.

> shared basin is an international one which must be jointly managed by the riparian states as a common resource for their equitable benefit helps create a common vision among the states, and encourages their cooperation and need to consult in managing the water resources for socio-economic development and the maintenance of environmental integrity anywhere in the basin.[34]

Accordingly, as in the rest of the world, collaboration in transboundary water management in West Africa is achieved gradually through water instruments that create rights and obligations of riparian states and establish a basin organization.[35] The history of benefit sharing and cooperation in the use of the shared water recourses is the cornerstone of stability and peace in the region.[36]

Though there is record of minimal activities on the shared watercourses in West Africa, the practice of regulating shared watercourses through adopting water regimes has progressed rapidly since 1990s (after independence), particularly after the adoption of the UN Watercourses Convention and the UNECE Water Convention. Most water treaties adopted in West Africa in the post-1990s were also inspired by these treaties.[37] Nevertheless, efforts in the region prior to adoption of the two UN treaties are worthy of recognition. Accordingly,

> Godana stressed that despite the gap between, on the one hand, the vast number of African international drainage basins and their potential for socio-economic development of the States and, on the other hand, the dearth of international regulations governing water resources,

34 Nii Boi Ayibotele, 'Senegal—Establishing a Transboundary Organisation for IWRM in the Senegal River Basin Case #45.' (n.d.), https://brucehooper.files.wordpress.com/2016/10/transboundary-establishing-a-transboundary-organisation-for-iwrm-in-the-senegal-river-basin-45.pdf. (accessed 26 January 2017).

35 Komlan Sangbana, "La Gestion Intégrée des Ressources en eaux Partagées et les Organismes de Bassin en Afrique: Les cas de l'Autorité du Bassin du Niger et de l'Autorité du Bassin de la Volta" in Société Français pour le Droit International, *L'eau en droit International, Colloque de Orléans*–(Paris, A. Pedone, 2011).

36 United Nations,' Water resources, A reason for Cooperation Not Conflict'. *United Nations News Centre* (22 November 2016), http://www.un.org/apps/news/story.asp?NewsID=55626#.WFFeUrIrLIU. (accessed 14 December 2014)

37 The preambles to the Niger Basin Water Charter, the Charter of Waters of the Senegal River, and the Water Charter of the Lake Chad Basin recognize the importance of both the UN Watercourses Convention and the UNECE water Convention.

> it was noteworthy that the achievements in terms of cooperation were impressive.[38]

Transboundary water governance in West Africa can be analyzed in three stages: the colonial instruments that served the Europeans; post-colonial before 1990 instruments; and the post-1990 instruments that emerged after the adoption of the UNECE Water Convention and the UN Watercourses Convention. Before turning to a more fulsome discussion of the post-1990 instruments in subsequent sections, the colonial and post-colonial before 1990 instruments will be reviewed below.

1.2.1 Colonial Water Regimes

The General Act of Berlin which was applicable to the Niger River,[39] was in force until it was replaced by the Convention Revising the General Act of Berlin and the General Act and Declaration of Brussels.[40] The regime was composed of six chapters and thirty eight articles. The eight articles of Chapter Five, titled Act of Navigation for the Niger, primarily regulated transportation along the Niger River and its tributaries and to that extent could be considered a basin agreement. The Preamble to the General Act of Berlin made applicable in West and Central Africa the principles of the Final Act of Congress of Vienna adopted in 1815. Though the Act of Congress of Vienna provided freedom of navigation to riparian states, the General Act of Berlin adopted the same principle for non-riparian states, namely, Europeans.[41] Its primary aim was to allow the Europeans easy access into West Africa in order to colonize the region and to freely move within the area they had acquired. Under this instrument, "the navigation of the Niger without excepting any of its branches and outlets is and shall remain entirely free for all merchant ships of all nations ... for transportation of goods and passengers."[42]

38 Mbengue (n 6) at 59 (abstract).

39 The General Act of Berlin was signed by representatives of the United Kingdom, France, Germany, Austria, Belgium, Denmark, Spain, the United States of America, Italy, the Netherlands, Portugal, Russia, Sweden-Norway, and Turkey (Ottoman Empire) in 1884.

40 The General Act of Berlin is divided into six titled chapters: Freedom of Trade in the Basin of the Congo; the Slave Trade; Neutrality of the Territories in the Basin of the Congo; Navigation of the Congo; Navigation of the Niger; and the Rules for Future Occupation on the Coast of the African Continent.

41 Salman (n 2) The Congress of Vienna was convened from 18 September 1814 to 9 June 1815; the Final Act of the Congress of Vienna, which is a collection of different treaties, was signed on 9 June 1815.

42 General Act of Berlin, art. 26.

The General Act of Berlin, which served the purposes of the colonial powers is flawed for several reasons. The instrument gave control of the river and enforcement of safety to different colonial powers depending on the part of the river that fell within their respective sovereignty or colonized territory without co-ordination.[43] Like its forerunner, the Berlin West African Congress, it did not accord any right or recognition to riparian local communities. They were not 'signatory powers.' The General Act of Berlin was actually "primarily intended to demonstrate the agreement of the Powers with regard to the general principles which should guide their commercial and civilizing action in the little known or inadequately organised regions of a continent…."[44] Finally, apart from Niger River, the regime failed to recognize other major rivers in West Africa. However, another treaty, the Convention and Statute on Freedom of Transit (the Barcelona Convention) provided for navigation on the Niger River and other major rivers in West Africa.[45]

The General Act of Berlin was replaced by the Convention Revising the General Act of Berlin and the General Act of Declaration of Brussels (the 1919 Convention), which comprised of fifteen articles. It was made applicable to the two river basins defined by Article 1 of the General Act of Berlin namely the Niger River Basin in West Africa and Congo River in East Africa.[46] Articles 5 and 6 of the instrument opened the rivers for navigation to all signatory powers and members of the League of Nation, not just particular colonial powers.[47] As observed with the earlier treaty, riparian communities in the region of Africa referred to as 'natives,' were not aware of the regime. Apart from navigation and commercial activities, the General Act of Berlin, the 1919 Convention and the Barcelona Convention failed to consider other uses of the shared watercourses. Moreover, the treaties were contracted by non-riparian colonists for their benefit and could not be said to have achieved cooperation

43 General Act of Berlin, art. 30. Articles 17 to 21 of the Act established the International Commission of Navigation of the Congo Basin, but no such organization was created for the Niger River Basin.

44 Convention Revising the General Act of Berlin and the General Act of Declaration of Brussels, preamble.

45 Convention and Statute on Freedom of Transit, Barcelona, 20 April 1921, preamble http://treaties.fco.gov.uk/docs/fullnames/pdf/1923/TS0027%20(1923)%20CMD-1992%201921%2020%20APR,%20BARCELONA%3B%20CONVENTION%20&%20STATUTE%20ON%20FREEDOM%20OF%20TRANSIT.pdf. (accessed 18 January 2017).

46 Convention Revising the General Act of Berlin and the General Act of Declaration of Brussels, art. 1.

47 The League of Nations was formed on 10 January 1920 after World War I as an association of nations to provide a forum for resolution of international disputes.

in the use of the transboundary watercourse in the sense recognized in international water law today.

Apart from these three regimes, no other legal regime or activity referred to the Niger River at this time except for the *Office du Niger* established by French colonial power in 1932 in Mali for agriculture.[48] In the Volta River Basin, the history of transboundary water related agreement started in 1906 when Great Britain and France signed the Exchange of Notes between France and Great Britain relative to the Boundary between the Gold Coast and French Soudan and the Agreement between France and Great Britain relative to the frontier between French and British possessions from the Gulf of Guinea to the Niger (Southern Nigeria and Dahomey).[49] The agreements were for territorial division and cross-border native access not for the regulation of use of water resources. As noted above, in the Senegal River Basin there is record of colonial transboundary water activities in 1935 with creation of the OAV and the MAS.[50] Mbengue quoting Godana also noted that, in 1949 the French government established the *Commission consultative des études pour l'aménagement du fleuve Sénégal* composed of the Secretary-General of the General Government of French West Africa, the governors of Senegal, Mauritania and Sudan (Mali), four parliamentarians from each state, and the chiefs of public works of these countries "to examine the projects of harnessing the river for purposes of navigation, hydro-electric power production, irrigation and agricultural production, as well as pastoralism."[51] Mbengue remarked that this instrument did not contribute to development of international water law.[52] However, according to Ayibotele, the setting up of a river basin organization for the Senegal River Basin in this era initiated a process of cooperation to develop that river basin on an integrated basis; this process blossomed after independence.[53]

1.2.2 Post-Colonial Era before 1990

Prior to 1990, the post colonial era was characterized by efforts to institute cooperation in the management of some major shared watercourses in West Africa because the independent states recognized the need for solidarity in

48 Salman (n 2).

49 Yongxuan Gao and Amy Margolies 'Transboundary Water Governance in the Volta River Basin' *Tufts Wikis*, (2009), https://wikis.uit.tufts.edu/confluence/display/aquapedia/Transboundary+Water+Governance+in+the+Volta+River+Basin. (accessed 16 January 2017).

50 Mbengue (n 6) at 60.

51 Ibid.

52 Ibid.

53 Ayibotele (n 34).

managing a common resource. Referring to the Niger River Basin, Salman remarks that the riparian states embarked on negotiations on the modalities for cooperation over the river soon after they attained independence in the early 1960s.[54] Six shared watercourses in the region that are the subject of some legal instruments within this period are the Senegal River Basin, the Niger River Basin, the Lake Chad Basin, the Gambia River Basin, the Volta River Basin, and Koliba-Korubal River Basin.

Senegal River Basin

Although Senegal River Basin Development Mission was set up in 1935, there was very limited achievement in management of the shared watercourse until the countries gained independence in the early 1960s. Between 1960 and 1980, the Senegal River Basin states contracted five important treaties: the Convention Relating to the General Development of the Senegal River (Bamako Convention); the Convention Concerning the Status of the Senegal River (Senegal River Basin Convention); the Convention Establishing the Organization for the Development of the Senegal River (OMVS Convention); the Convention Concerning the Legal Status of Common Works; and the Convention Regarding the Methods of Financing Joint Works.

The Bamako Convention is the first post-colonial indigenous water treaty in West Africa[55] and could be described as the forerunner of indigenous shared watercourse regimes in the region. Its aim was for integrated development of the Senegal River Basin and to rationally harness its various resources. To achieve these goals, Article 1 of the Convention established an Inter-State Committee "to promote and coordinate studies and development work on the Senegal River Basin."[56] Although the Convention did not lay down any direct principles of cooperation in the River Basin, it empowered the Inter-State Committee to decide and formulate programs for development of the Basin.[57] Ayibotele remarks that "under this Convention the Senegal River was declared an international water way in 1964 and an Inter-State Committee realized the need for the Senegal River to be accorded an international river status and

54 Salman (n 2).

55 The Convention Relating to the General Development of the Senegal River (Bamako Convention) was adopted on 26 July 1963 by the four riparian states of the Senegal River Basin: Senegal, Mauritania, Mali and Guinea.

56 Article 2 of the Bamako Convention states that the Inter-State Committee shall be composed of four members on the basis of one person per riparian state.

57 Bamako Convention, art. 8.

to regulate the river upstream by building a storage reservoir."[58] Generally, the Bamako Convention is a non-perfect regime and it lacks dispute settlement provisions. However, it started a process that led to a better system of cooperation and water treaty development in the Basin and in West Africa. The Inter-State Committee set to work and subsequently adopted a regional development plan for the Senegal River Basin that lasted for ten years (from 1963 to 1972). The development plan "defined the objectives, areas of emphasis to achieve the objectives, the productive activities to be promoted, the needs for regional and national economic integration and corresponding integrated management of the water resources."[59] To achieve this plan, the riparian states adopted the Convention Concerning the Status of the Senegal River (Senegal River Basin Convention) in 1972.[60]

The Senegal River Basin Convention recognized the Senegal River as an international river and a common resource to be managed jointly by all the riparian states. It was contracted the same day as the OMVS Convention.[61] Article 2 of the Senegal River Basin Convention reflects the principle of solidarity and cooperation as parties "declare willingness to develop close cooperation in order to operate rationally Senegal River resources and ensure freedom of navigation and equal treatment." Unlike the Bamako Convention, the Senegal River Basin Convention sets out binding obligations for contracting states, although substantive and procedural principles of international water law are not well enunciated. Article 4 forbids any project on the river that will alter the characteristics of the river, the health status of its waters, or the biological characteristics of its fauna and flora except with approval of other contracting parties. The OMVS Convention established the Organization for Development of the Senegal River, an organizational structure, and a "tool for establishing transboundary organization of water resources management" in the River Basin.[62] The institutional structure of the OMVS Convention recognized by the

58 Ayibotele (n 34) at 5. Previously, the Senegal River was described as inter-territorial not international because the entire basin was under French colonial rule.

59 Ibid.

60 Convention Concerning the Status of the Senegal River, Nouakchott, 11 March 1972 https://iea.uoregon.edu/treaty-text/1964-dakarsenegalriverbasinfrtxt. (accessed 11 January 2017).

61 Convention Establishing the Organization for the Development of the Senegal River (OMVS Convention), Nouakchott, 11 March 1972 https://iea.uoregon.edu/treaty-text/1964-dakarsenegalriverbasinfrtxt. (accessed 11 January 2017).

62 Ayibotele (n 34). The organisational structure of the Senegal River Basin comprises the Conference of Heads of State and Government, the Council of Ministers, the High Commission, co-ordination and consultative bodies, the OMVS Consultative Committee and the Permanent Water Commission.

most recent Charter of the Waters of Senegal River still operates in the Senegal River Basin.

The Convention concluded between Mali, Mauritania and Senegal Regarding the Legal Status of Common Works defines some basin projects as joint or common works and indivisible projects of all the Senegal River Basin member states.[63] According to Ayibotele, the aim of the treaty is to meet regional development needs of the states of the River Basin. To achieve this purpose, the projects are also jointly financed, constructed and managed by the river basin organization (the OMVS) as enabled by the Convention Regarding the Methods of Financing Joint Works.[64] The latter treaty was adopted to strengthen inter-state cooperation for the implementation of the program for the development of the Senegal River Basin and to define financing arrangement of common works.[65] Both conventions relating to common works are innovations in transboundary water resources management and also depict the solidarity of riparian states of the Senegal River Basin. They are the pioneer of similar instruments and provisions in the West Africa region regarding the principle of common works. Mbengue states that "never before had riparian states of an African international watercourse agreed through a conventional instrument to subject works on a shared watercourse to a regime of common and indivisible ownership."[66] Tignino and Sangbana opined that the Senegal River Basin regime on common works is "to date a unique example of cooperation in the use of the waters of an international watercourse for hydroelectric, agricultural and navigation purposes."[67]

---

63 Article 2 of the Convention concluded between Mali, Mauritania and Senegal Regarding the Legal Status of Common Works defined a common work as any work that is the subject of a legal instrument declaring the work to be common property. Article 3 defines such projects to include the Manantali Dam, the Diama Dam, the river seaport of Saint-Louis; the river port of Kayes; port stops and works for the development of the navigable channel; and ancillary works and accessories. Adopted 21 December 1978. https://iea.uoregon.edu/base-agreement-list/Senegal%20River%20Basin (accessed 16 January 2017).

64 Convention Regarding the Methods of Financing Joint Works, Bamako, 12 May 1982, https://iea.uoregon.edu/treaty-text/1982-senegalriverfinancingmodalitiescommonworksfrtxt. (accessed 30 August 2017).

65 Ibid., preamble. The common works are financed through contributions by member states, loans contracted by member states and lent to the OMVS, guaranteed or unguaranteed loans contracted by the OMVS, and grants and subsidies to the organization.

66 Mbengue (n 6) at 64.

67 M. Tignino & K. Sangbana "Le statut d'ouvrages communs et le partages des bénéfices dans les bassins du fleuve Sénégal et Niger". *Geneva Water Hub* (2016), pp. 1–7, https://archive-ouverte.unige.ch/unige:80736.

Niger River Basin

Unlike the Senegal River, the Niger River was subject of two water regimes before the post colonial era, though the instruments were not African in origin.[68] Like the Senegal River Basin, the Niger River Basin was governed by several regimes in the post-colonial era before 1990. The most important instruments are the Act of Niamey; the Agreement Concerning the Niger River Commission and the Navigation and Transport on the River Niger; Agreement Revising the Agreement Concerning the Niger River Commission and the Navigation and Transport on the River Niger; the Convention Creating the Niger Basin Authority; and the Revised Convention Creating the Niger Basin Authority. Although some Niger River Basin States adopted other treaties, they are not inclusive of all Basin states and therefore not considered here.[69]

The first indigenous water regime for cooperation in the Niger River Basin is the Act of Niamey which abolished the Act of Berlin as it concerns the Niger River and its tributaries.[70] Unlike the Bamako Convention, which was adopted same year, the Act of Niamey defines the principle of cooperation in the use of the water resources of the Niger River Basin. Article 2 opened use of the Niger River and its tributaries to all riparian states "for navigation, agricultural, industrial uses and collection of the products of its fauna and flora." Contracting states were also obliged to cooperate on the study and execution of any project that could affect appreciably the regime of the Niger River and "the biological characteristics of its fauna and flora."[71] Although this provision is broad, the Act of Niamey is the first instrument in West Africa to recognize the need for parties to cooperate and exchange information on any project that could affect a river basin and this was done long before the Helsinki Rules on the Uses of the Waters of International Rivers were adopted.[72] The Act of Niamey

68 The regimes are the General Act of Berlin and the Convention Revising the General Act of Berlin and the General Act and Declaration of Brussels, which are above.

69 Examples include the Bilateral Agreement Between the Federal Republic of Nigeria and the Republic of Niger Concerning the Equitable Sharing in the Development, Conservation and Use of their Common Water Resource adopted 18 July 1990, and the Protocol of the Agreement Between the Republic of Niger and the Republic of Mali Relative to Cooperation in the Utilisation of Resources in Water of the Niger River, adopted 12 July 1988. See Amidou Garane et al. 'West Africa' F. Loures & *A. Rieu Clarke* (eds), *The UN Watercourses Convention in Force: Strengthening International Law For Transboundary Water Management* (London Rouledge, 2013) at 100.

70 Act of Niamey, art. 1.

71 Ibid., art. 4.

72 The Helsinki Rules on the uses of Waters of International River were adopted by the International Law Association in August 1966. http://www.internationalwaterlaw.org/documents/intldocs/helsinki_rules.htm (accessed 13 January 2017).

also established an 'Inter-Governmental Organisation' for further cooperation and for encouraging, promoting, and co-coordinating studies and programs concerning exploitation of the resources of the River Basin.[73] It also provided for settlement of disputes regarding the interpretation and application of the treaty, provisions that are absent in the Bamako Convention.[74]

The Act of Niamey was supplemented by the Agreement Concerning the Niger River Commission and the Navigation and Transport on the River Niger (1964 NRC Agreement) which defined the Inter-Governmental Organization under Article 5 of the Niamey Act as the Niger River Commission.[75] The instrument also sets out the composition of the Niger River Commission and its major functions which primarily are the application of the principles of the Act and liaising between basin states. To achieve cooperation on matters under Article 4 of the Act, the 1964 NRC Agreement provides that the riparian states must early inform the Commission,

> of all studies and works upon which they propose to embark. They undertake further to abstain from carrying out on the portion of the River, its tributaries and sub-tributaries subject to their jurisdiction any works likely to pollute the waters, or any modification likely to affect biological characteristics of its fauna and flora, without adequate notice to, and prior consultation with, the Commission.[76]

This provision creates a binding obligation regarding planned project in the Basin and further dispenses with the loose provision of Article 4 of the Act of Niamey.

---

73 Although, Article 5 of the Act of Niamey established an inter-governmental organization, its composition was the "subject of subsequent agreement."

74 Article 7 of the Act of Niamey provides that "any dispute that may arise between the riparian States regarding the interpretation or application of the present Act shall be amicably settled by direct agreement between them or through the Inter-Governmental Organisation referred to in Articles 5 and 6 above. Failing such settlement, the dispute shall be decided by arbitration, in particular by the Commission of Mediation, Conciliation and Arbitration of the Organisation of African Unity, or by judicial settlement by the International Court of Justice."

75 Agreement Concerning the Niger River Commission and the Navigation and Transport on the River Niger, Niamey, 25 November 1964, art. 1, https://iea.uoregon.edu/treaty-text/1964-nigerrivercommissionnavigationtransportrivernigerentxt (accessed 30 August 2017).

76 Ibid., art. 12.

The 1964 NRC Agreement was modified and replaced by the Agreement Revising the Agreement Concerning the Niger River Commission and the Navigation and Transport on the River Niger (1973 NRC Agreement).[77] Under Article 4 of the 1973 NRC Agreement, the Niger River Commission could make requests and enter into agreements for financial and technical assistance "provided that such agreements involving financial obligations from Member States shall become binding only after approval by the Member States concerned." It also reinforced the provision in the 1964 NRC Agreement that the Commission must not only be informed of studies and works, but that such works likely to pollute the waters or change the biological characteristics of fauna and flora of the Niger River Basin must only be done with prior notice and consultation of the Commission.[78]

In 1980, the Niger River Commission was re-named the Niger Basin Authority in the Convention Creating the Niger Basin Authority (NBA Convention), which also revised all the previous instruments except the Act of Niamey.[79] Under the NBA Convention, the functions of the Niger River Commission were modified and adopted by the Niger Basin Authority. Article 3 of the Convention defines the purpose of the Authority as follows:

> to promote the co-operation among member States and to ensure an integrated development of the Niger Basin in all fields, by developing its resources particularly in the fields of energy, water resources, agriculture, animal husbandry, fishing and fisheries, forestry and forestry exploitation, transport, communications and industry.

It will also harmonize the national development policies in the Basin through the implementation of integrated development of projects and programs.[80] The NBA Convention is remarkable because it marked 'progression' from emphasis on river to the concept of river basin. Hence, the Convention was adopted

77 Adopted 15 June 1973 (1973 NRC agreement) https://iea.uoregon.edu/treaty-text/1973-amendments-1964-nigerrivercommissionnavigationtransportrivernigerentxt (accessed 13 January 2017).

78 Ibid., art. 5.

79 Convention Creating the Niger Basin Authority (NBA Convention), Faranah, 21 November 1980. https://iea.uoregon.edu/treaty-text/1980-nigerbasinauthorityentxt (accessed 13 January 2017). Article 21 of the NBA Convention provides that "this Convention revises the Niamey Agreement, signed in Niamey on the 25th of November 1964 revised in Niamey on the 2nd February 1968 and on the 15th June 1973, and in Lagos on the 26th January 1979."

80 Ibid., art. 3.

to achieve integrated management in the Niger River Basin. Though the NBA Convention was revised by the Revised Convention Creating the Niger Basin Authority,[81] the Act of Niamey remained the principal instrument for regulation of shared water resources of the Niger River Basin until it was replaced by the Niger Basin Water Charter in 2008.[82]

Lake Chad Basin

For decades, the main instrument for regulation of the Lake Chad Basin was the Convention and Statutes Relating to the Development of the Chad Basin (Fort Lamy Convention).[83] The regime codified binding obligations on the state parties, but its most important feature was the creation of a basin organization, the Lake Chad Basin Commission (LCBC) with defined functions. The LCBC, which still operates today, is the earliest basin organization in West Africa established under the same regime that regulates the shared watercourse.[84] This is unlike the Inter-State Committee of the Bamako Convention, which is without defined functions, and the Inter-Governmental Organisation of the Act of Niamey, which was made subject to a future agreement. The Fort Lamy Convention also created a dispute resolution process, which must be commenced through the Commission unlike the provisions of the Act of Niamey.[85]

The main obligation on the state parties under the Fort Lamy Convention was

> not to undertake in that part of the Basin within their jurisdiction any work in connection with the development of water resources … likely to have a marked influence upon the system of the water resources and levels of the Basin without adequate notice and prior consultations with the Commission …[86]

---

81 Revised Convention Creating the Niger Basin Authority, N'djamena, 27 October 1987. https://iea.uoregon.edu/treaty-text/1987-revised-1980-nigerbasinauthorityfrtxt. (accessed 17 January 2017).

82 Niger Basin Water Charter, Niamey, 30 April 2008. https://iea.uoregon.edu/treaty-text/2008-nigerbasinwatercharterfrtxt. (accessed17 January 2007).

83 Convention and Statutes Relating to the Development of the Chad Basin, Fort lamy, 22 May 1964. https://iea.uoregon.edu/treaty-text/1964-developmentchadbasin conventionentxt. (accessed 15 January 2017).

84 Ibid., art. 1.

85 Ibid., art. 7. Article 7 of the Niamey Act allows the parties to negotiate settlement directly or through the Inter-Governmental Organisation that later became the Niger River Commission.

86 Fort Lamy Convention, art. 5.

This was an improvement on the loose provisions in the Act of Niamey.[87] Article 4 of the Fort Lamy Convention addressed "utilization of the surface and underground waters" of the Chad Basin and was the earliest indication of a treaty that covered both surface water and groundwater of a transboundary watercourse in West Africa. Although Garane observes that this provision is unclear and subject to the argument that it does not directly include aquifers of the Basin but is relevant for the purposes of integrated basin management, the provision stands out in an era where most regimes stressed surface water.[88] Recently, riparian states adopted the Water Charter for the Lake Chad Basin to replace the Fort Lamy Convention.[89]

Gambia River Basin

The first instrument adopted for the Gambia River Basin is the Convention Creating the Co-ordinating Committee of the Gambia River Basin.[90] This regime did not last long and was replaced by the Convention Relating to the Status of the River Gambia (Gambia River Basin Convention) and the Convention Relating to the Creation of the Gambia River Basin Development Organization (OMVG Convention).[91] The regimes are similar to regimes of the Senegal River Basin and both river basin organizations were established to promote cooperation in the basins and to implement the provisions of the treaties.[92] However, Article 4 of the Gambia River Basin Convention is unique because it provides that projects that impact the characteristics of the Basin's fauna and flora must not be implemented without prior approval of all contracting parties and "such approval should be received within six month. Beyond this deadline the State concerned may as of right proceed with execution of

87 Article 4 of the Niamey Act only encourages party states to study and cooperate on any project.

88 Garane (n 27).

89 Water Charter for the Lake Chad Basin, N'djamena, 13 April 2012. https://www.africanwaterfacility.org/fileadmin/uploads/awf/Projects/MULTIN-LAKECHAD-Water-Charter.pdf (accessed 7 September 2017).

90 The Convention creating the Co-ordinating Committee of the Gambia River Basin was adopted 16 April 1976. See 'Joint Management of Transboundary Water Resources: The OMVG Experience,' *Gambia River Basin Development Organization.* http://strategicforesight.com/conference_pdf/Presentation%20by%20OMVG.pdf. (accessed 14 January 2017).

91 Both regimes were in adopted in Kaolack, 30 June 1980. http://iea.uoregon.edu/base-agreement-list/Gambia%20River. (accessed 13 January 2017).

92 Convention Concerning the Status of the Senegal River, art. 11: Convention Relating to Status of River Gambia, art. 11.

its project."[93] Prior to adoption of the Gambia River Basin Convention no instrument in the region placed any time limit within which a state could seek approval for any planned project. More recent water treaties in the region recognize the importance of this provision which is also consistent with Article 13 of the UN Watercourses Convention.[94] Another difference between the Gambia River Basin Convention and the Senegal River Basin regime is that Article 1 of the Convention Concerning the Status of the Senegal River declares the Senegal River an international river, while the Gambia River with its tributaries is declared a river of regional interest.[95] The compositions of the river basin organizations (OMVS and OMVG respectively) are also slightly different.[96] Like the Senegal River Basin States, the Gambia River Basin States also adopted the Convention on the Legal Status of Common Structures[97] which defines the 'legal status of common structures and the rights and obligation of co-owners.'[98] Further basin agreements have been adopted to amend these Conventions.[99]

93 Article 4 of the Convention Concerning the Status of the Senegal River provides that such projects must be with the approval of contracting parties without providing a time frame of such approval.

94 Article 13 of the UN Watercourses Convention provides for a six-month period for notification of planned measures but Article 20 of the Niger Basin Water Charter and Article 24 of the Charter of Waters of the Senegal River provide for a three month notification period. Article 55 of the Water Charter of the Lake Chad Basin recognizes a four months period.

95 Convention Relating to the Status of the River Gambia, art. 1.

96 Although both organizations have similar institutional structure, Article 7 of the Senegal Water Convention excludes the Conference of Heads of State and Government as part of its permanent organs while Article 3 of the Convention Relating to the Creation of the Gambia River Basin Organization includes the Conference of Heads Of State And Government as a permanent body of the OMVG.

97 The Convention on the Legal Status of Common Structure was adopted 29 June 1985. Available at the headquarters of the OMVG, Koalack, Senegal. Information about this regime in public domain is limited but it is briefly reported in 'Joint Management of Transboundary Water Resources: The OMVG Experience,' *Gambia River Basin Development Organization.* (n 90).

98 Ibid. (n 90).

99 They are Amendment of Article 4 To The Convention Relating To The Status Of The River Gambia amended by Resolution 5/CEG/CG of 5 June 1981 of the Conference of Heads of State and Government; Amendment To The Convention Relating To The Creation Of The Gambia River Basin Development Organization and the Convention Relating To The Status Of The River Gambia (Adhesion of Guinée) by virtue of Resolution 2/CEG/CG of 6 June 1981 of the Conference of Heads of State and Government of the Gambia River Basin

Koliba-Korubal River Basin

The only regime for the Koliba-Korubal River Basin is the Protocol of the Agreement between Republic of Guinea and Republic of Guinea Bissau on the Management of River Koliba-Korubal (Koliba-Korubal River Basin Protocol),[100] a brief treaty with only eight articles. Its preamble declares that the intention of parties is to 'preserve solidarity,' hence the need to optimize integrated development of Koliba-Korubal River Basin "without prejudice to the interests of each country."[101] The Protocol established a river basin organization, the Permanent Technical Committee, for implementing its main objectives, which are defined in Article 2. Although the composition of the Permanent Technical Committee is defined, it reports to an undefined Joint Cooperation Committee.[102] The Koliba-Korubal regime has been criticized for its "complete absence of specific rules and procedures to facilitate, guide and inform the work of the technical committee the agreement creates."[103] The dispute resolution requirement in the regime is also very weak because it provides for dispute resolution through 'amicable settlement' by the parties.[104] However, the Kolibal-Korubal River Basin regime precedes the UN Watercourses Convention and was also adopted before any regime was put in place for the Volta River Basin.[105] The Kolibal-Korubal River Basin is better served than others in West Africa without specific basin agreements.

Development Organization; Amendment Of The Preamble To The Convention Relating To The Creation Of The Gambia River Basin Development Organization by Resolution 4/CEG/CG of 6 June 1981; Amendment Of Articles 17 and 18 To The Convention Relating To The Creation Of The Gambia River Basin Development Organization by Resolution 6/CEG/CG of 6 June 1981 of the Conference of Heads of State and Government; Amendment To The Convention Relating To The Creation Of The Gambia River Basin Development Organization (Adhesion of Guinée-Bissau) by Resolution no 9/CEG 5/DS of 7 July 1983.

100 Conakry, 21 October, 1978 (Koliba-Korubal River Basin Protocol). http://gis.nacse.org/tfdd/tfdddocs/403FRE.pdf (accessed 30 August 2017).

101 Koliba-Korubal River Basin Protocol, art. 1.

102 The Permanent Technical Committee is composed of Representatives of government of both countries; heads of teams operating in the field; representatives of national technical services in both countries; and representatives of donor agencies.

103 Garane (n 27).

104 Koliba-Korubal River Basin Protocol, art. 8.

105 The first water regime for the Volta River Basin, the Convention on the Status of the Volta River and the Establishment of Volta Basin Authority, was adopted in Ouagadougou on 19 January 2007.

The Volta River Basin

The Volta River Basin is the second largest basin in West Africa.[106] Nevertheless, unlike the Niger River and other major shared watercourses in the region, the Volta River Basin witnessed very little effort regarding regulation of its use in the post-colonial era. According to Gao and Margolies, "there has been little coordinated transboundary effort in the basin until recently."[107] The only instrument that affected the Basin within the post-colonial era before 1990 is the Agreement Governing the Operations of Onchocerciasis Control Program in the Volta River Basin.[108] Although signed by the six riparian states, "this cooperative effort was limited to control of water borne disease (onchocerciasis or river blindness), not water sharing or management."[109] The first major water regime of the Volta River Basin is the Code of Conduct of Conduct for Sustainable and Equitable Management of Shared Water Resources of the Volta Basin adopted by Ghana and Burkina Faso.[110] Further developments in the Basin are the establishment of the Volta Basin Authority in 2006 and the adoption of the first Basin treaty, the Convention on the Status of the Volta River and Establishment of the Volta Basin Authority in 2007.

The early West Africa water treaties were not influenced by any UN water treaty because there was none. They were driven by the desire of riparian states to cooperate in the management of the shared water resources. They have defined scope and also recognize the principle of notification, but do not reflect the modern substantive principles of international water law such as equitable and reasonable utilization, protection of ecosystems, and the obligation not to cause significant harm. Nevertheless, most of them were innovative regimes. While few transboundary water systems in West Africa have instruments for

---

106 The six riparian states of Volta River Basin are Ghana, Burkina Faso, Côte d'Ivoire, Mali, Togo and Benin. It lies next to the Niger River Basin, which has nine riparian states (Nigeria, Niger, Benin, Mali, Burkina Faso, Guinea, Cameroon, Chad and Côte d'Ivoire).

107 Gao and Margolies (n 49).

108 The Onchocerciasis Control Program Agreement was an initiative of the World Health Organization (WHO), World Bank, United Nations Development Programme (UNDP) and Food and Agriculture Organisation of the United Nations (FAO). See Agreement Governing the Operations of the Onchocerciasis Control Programme in the Volta River Basin Area, Accra, 1, November 1973. http://www.internationalwaterlaw.org/documents/regionaldocs/1973_Agreement_on_Onchocerciasis_Control_Programme_in_the_Volta_River_Basin_area-English.pdf. (accessed 16 January 2017).

109 Gao and Margolies (n 49).

110 The Volta Basin Code of Conduct was adopted by Ghana and Burkina Faso in July 2006. http://www.dialoguebarrages.net/fr/ressources-et-documents/doc_download/122-niger-basin-authority-nba-water-code. (accessed 30 August 2017).

management of shared watercourses and a host of others lack any form of governance, it is suggested that application of the principles set out in the UN Watercourses Convention and the UNECE Water Convention could add value to shared watercourses management in West Africa.[111] The Conventions would then serve as suppletory norms to the treaty regimes in the region and provide needed regulation for basins without treaties. This raises other questions that are considered in the sections below: Since the region had established a good history of adopting regimes for managing some of the shared watercourses before the UN Watercourses Convention and the UNECE Water Convention were adopted, does it still need both UN water treaties? Would a region based treaty be preferable or should river basins be encouraged to adopt their own basin-specific instruments?

2.0 Understanding the 1997 UN Watercourses Convention and the 1992 UNECE Water Convention

The UN Watercourses Convention was adopted as a global instrument for the regulation and management of shared watercourses (for non-navigational uses). It has been described as the only universal treaty governing shared freshwater resources[112] and "its adoption by the UN General Assembly on May 21, 1997 marked an historic moment in the evolution of international water law."[113] The UN Watercourses Convention is a framework convention because its principles and rules could be adjusted to fit into circumstances and peculiarities of different international shared watercourses. It does not exclude the rights and obligations of states arising out of existing or several watercourses' agreements, or their right to choose to reconcile the provisions of such agreements with those of the UN Watercourses Convention.[114] Although existing treaties do not have to be altered, they could be harmonized to conform to the

111 ECOWAS et al. (n 24) at 4.

112 Stephen C. McCaffrey 'Convention on the Law of Non–navigational Uses of International Watercourses', *United Nations Audio-visual Library of International Law* http://legal.un.org/avl/ha/clnuiw/clnuiw.html (accessed 15 January 2017).

113 Salman M.A. Salman, 'The United Nations Watercourses Convention Ten Years Later—Why Has its Entry into Force Proven Difficult?' *Water International*, Vol. 32, No. 1 (2007), pp. 1–15, http://www.unwatercoursesconvention.org/images/2012/10/Salman-UNWatercoursesConventionTenYears.pdf. (accessed 15 January 2017).

114 Article 3(1) of the UN Watercourses Convention recognizes existing rights and obligations arising from other agreements in force on the date a state become party to the Convention.

provisions of the UN Watercourses Convention. Also, states are encouraged to consider its provisions when adopting new treaties.[115] According to Wouters, the UN Watercourses Convention "is a global framework agreement with the goal to ensure the utilization, development, conservation, management and protection of international watercourses and the promotion of their optimal and sustainable utilisation for present and future generations."[116]

The UNECE Water Convention was adopted as a regional treaty "to strengthen national measures and international cooperation for the ecologically sound management and protection of transboundary surface waters and ground waters."[117] It is also a framework convention adopted to

> lay down certain general principles and requirements for its parties to be further developed and made operational through the adoption of subsequent protocols and certain non-binding (soft laws) instruments in the form of guidelines and recommendations on specific subjects within the Convention.[118]

Unlike the provisions in the UN Watercourses Convention, riparian states are obliged to conform their treaties to the text of the Convention which creates some general obligations for party states and specific obligations for riparian states.[119]

2.1 *Scope*

Article 1 of the UNECE Water Convention defines transboundary waters as "any surface or ground waters which mark, cross or are located on boundaries

---

115 'According to Abseno, "the positive contributions of…. UN Watercourses Convention can be used to inspire the development of a basin-wide framework in other international watercourse agreements". M. M. Abseno 'The Influence of the UN Watercourses Convention on the Development of a Treaty Regime in the Nile River Basin' *Water International*, Vol. 38, No. 2, (March 2003), pp. 192–203 at 201.

116 Wouters. (n 28).

117 UNECE, *Guide to Implementing the Water Convention*, (New York and Geneva, United Nations, 2013), preface.

118 Ibid. at 9.

119 Article 9 of the UNECE Water Convention provides that "the Riparian Parties shall on the basis of equality and reciprocity enter into bilateral or multilateral agreements or other arrangements, where these do not yet exist, or adapt existing ones, where necessary to eliminate the contradictions with the basic principles of this Convention, in order to define their mutual relations and conduct regarding the prevention, control and reduction of transboundary impact."

between two or more States…." Though the concepts of 'international' and 'transboundary' are similar, the definition of 'transboundary waters' in the UNECE Water Convention is not exactly the same as the definition of 'international watercourse' in the UN Watercourses Convention.[120] Article 2 of the UN Watercourses Convention defines watercourse as "a system of surface waters and ground waters constituting by virtue of their physical relationship a unitary whole and normally flowing into a common terminus" and defines an international watercourse as "a watercourse, parts of which are situated in different states." Lipper explains that an international river is either a successive river (river flowing through the territory of more than one state) or a boundary river (river separating the territories of two states.)[121] In the UNECE Water Convention, transboundary waters cover both surface waters and groundwaters, while 'international watercourse' in the UN Watercourses Convention refers to surface water and ground water that is hydrological connected with the surface water. The restrictive definition of watercourse in the UN Watercourses Convention excludes transboundary confined aquifers which are covered by the UNECE Water Convention.

The definition of watercourse in the UN Watercourses Convention is similar to the definition of 'international drainage basin' in the Helsinki Rules on the Uses of the Waters of International Rivers.[122] Article 11 of the Helsinki Rules defines an international drainage basin as "a geographical area extending over two or more states determined by the watershed limits of the system of waters, including surface and underground waters, flowing into a common terminus". Although the Helsinki Rules apply to groundwater connected to surface water, the concept of drainage basin is wider than the concept of international watercourse.[123] The position of the UN Watercourses Convention seems to favor regulation of use of the water to the exclusion of the land territory. However, in a situation where activities in the land affect the water, Article 20 of the Convention, which provides for "protection and preservation of ecosystem," becomes relevant. It suggests that, geographically the UN Watercourses

120 Although the title of UNECE Water Convention includes both 'transboundary watercourse' and 'international lakes' the scope of the Convention is different from that of the UN Watercourses Convention.

121 Jerome Lipper 'Equitable Utilisation' *in* H. A Garretson et al. (eds) *The Law of International Drainage Basins* (New York, Oceana Publications, 1967) at 16.

122 Helsinki Rules (n 72), art. 2.

123 The term, drainage basin covers the whole drainage area of the river including the land, watershed, all the tributaries and confluence of the river; a watercourse is the channel which the river or body of water follows.

Convention also covers the entire river basin including land-based activities.[124] Similarly, the UNECE Water Convention also covers the entire drainage basin of the international watercourse because Article 2(6) of the Convention obliges riparian states to control pollution in the "relevant catchment areas."[125] Article 1 of the UN Watercourses Convention limits the scope of the Convention to the use of international watercourses for non-navigation purposes only. Though the UNECE Water Convention is silent on whether the Convention applies to both navigation and non-navigational uses, it appears to apply to all uses of the transboundary water, including navigation. Nevertheless, it does not include specific provisions on navigation as in the Helsinki Rules.[126]

2.2 *Substantive Rules*

International water law recognizes two types of substantive rules. The first comprises rules of customary international water law such as the principle of equitable and reasonable utilization and the obligation not to cause significant harm (popularly known as the 'no harm rule'); the second are the emerging substantive rules like protection of aquatic ecosystems and the human right to water.

Generally, the UN Watercourses Convention seems to codify substantive provisions better than the UNECE Water Convention because the principle of equitable and reasonable utilization is more clearly enunciated in the UN Watercourses Convention. According to Rieu-Clarke and Kinna, "the way in which the substantive norms are presented differs between both instruments."[127] Further, "the UNECE Water Convention provisions are generally more detailed or prescriptive than those of the UN Watercourses Convention. This is particularly the case regarding water quality standards as well as setting out more

124 Rieu-Clarke et al. (n 17) at 78.

125 The implication is that the UNECE Water Convention is a basin management instrument, which is linked to the principle of integrated water resources management (IWRM) covering both the watercourse and land activities.

126 Chapter 4 of the Helsinki Rules (Articles 12 to 20) codifies specific provisions on navigation. According to the United Nations Department of Economic and Social Affairs (UNDESA), "the focus of negotiation and treaty-making in the last century has shifted away from navigation towards the use, development, protection and conservation of water resources". 'Transboundary Waters,' *UNDSEA*, http://www.un.org/waterforlife decade/transboundary_waters.shtml (accessed 30 March 2017).

127 Alistair Rieu-Clarke and Rémy Kinna, 'Can Two Global UN Water Conventions Effectively Co-exist? Making the Case for a "Package Approach" to Support Institutional Coordination'. *Review of European, Comparative & International Environmental Law*, Vol. 23, No. 1 (April 2014), pp. 15–31.

precise guidelines and advanced standards of conduct for the prevention of transboundary impacts."[128] Tanzi seems to agree with this observation; in his opinion, at first sight, the UN Watercourses Convention seems to devote more attention to the substantive principles than the UNECE Water Convention, but on the whole, the 'General Principles' in Article 2 of the UNECE Water Convention set out the substantive provisions very concisely and reflect the normative content of the principles of equitable and reasonable utilization and the no harm rule without giving priority to either.[129] Salman is also of the view that the UN Watercourses Convention subordinates the no harm rule principle to the principles of equitable and reasonable utilization.[130] However, other water law experts do not accept this position. According to Wouters and Vinogradov, the UNECE Water Convention "contains a cursory reference to the need to ensure that transboundary waters are utilized in an equitable and reasonable way, but does not go beyond that."[131] Rieu-Clarke and Wouters further note that the UNECE Water Convention emphasizes the no harm rule but the UN Watercourses Convention creates "a duty of due diligence in the prevention of transboundary harm, incorporates the ecosystem approach, and provides for environmental protection and sustainable use of transboundary water resources, all around the central principle of equitable and reasonable

128 United Nations, 'UN Watercourses Convention and the UNECE Water Convention,' UN Watercourses Convention User's Guide Fact Sheet Series No. 12, http://www.unwatercoursesconvention.org/documents/UNWC-Fact-Sheet-12-Relationship-with-UNECE-Water-Convention.pdf (accessed 9 January 2017).

129 Atilla Tanzi 'The Relationship between the 1992 UNECE Convention on the Protection and Use of Transboundary Watercourses and International Lakes and the 1997 UN Convention on the Law of the Non Navigational Uses of International Watercourses'. Report of the UNECE Task Force on Legal and Administrative Aspects. *UNECE* (Geneva, February 2000), http://www.unece.org/fileadmin/DAM/env/water/publications/documents/conventiontotal.pdf (accessed 9 January 2017).

130 According to Salman M.A. Salman, an analysis of the provisions of Articles 5 and 6 of UN Watercourses Convention (equitable and reasonable utilization) and Article 7(2) of the UN Watercourses Convention suggest that "causing of harm may be tolerated in certain cases such as when the possibility of compensation may be considered". 'The Future of International Water Law: Regional Approaches to Shared Watercourses?,' *in* M. H. Arsanjani, J. K. Cogan, R. D. Sloane and S. Wiessner (eds), *Looking to the Future: Essays on International Law in Honor of W. Michael Reisman*, pp. 907–28 (The Hague, Martinus Nijhoff Publishers, (2011), http://www.salmanmasalman.org/wp-content/uploads/2012/12/ReismanBookChapter3-1.pdf (accessed 11 January 2017).

131 Patricia Wouters & Sergei Vinogradov, 'Analysing the ECE Water Convention: What Lessons for the Regional Management of Transboundary Water Resources'. *Yearbook of International Co-operation on Environment and Development* (2003/04), pp. 55–63.

use."[132] Some commentators favor the reasoning that the adoption of the UNECE Water Convention as a regional treaty created the basis for it to be more detailed than the UN Watercourses Convention, which is a global instrument, from the onset.[133] According to Subedi, the UN Watercourses Convention embodies the basic principles for utilization of an international watercourse but "the provisions need to be fleshed out to provide a comprehensive legal regime both for utilization and management of water as a valuable resource."[134] In spite of this position, the UN Watercourses Convention is more detailed in certain substantive provisions because it "places all substantive provisions under the overarching requirement that States utilize their international watercourses in an equitable and reasonable manner."[135]

2.2.1 Principle of Equitable and Reasonable Utilization

According to McCaffrey, the principle of equitable and reasonable utilization is the fundamental rule governing the use of international watercourses and is also the cornerstone of UN Watercourses Convention.[136] Arbitrary political division of an international watercourse generates an international problem of satisfying the competing interests of each state located within the basin. This raises two important questions for determining utilization of an international watercourse: Does a co-basin State have the right to use the waters? If the answer is 'yes,' what is the nature and extent of the right?[137] McCaffrey states that the equitable and reasonable utilization principle is a doctrine that governs allocation or apportionment of water through accommodating competing

132 Alistair Rieu-Clarke, Patricia Wouters and Flavia Loures, 'The Role and Relevance of the UN Convention on the Non-navigational Uses of International Watercourses to the EU and its Member States'. *Centre for Water Law, Policy and Science, University of Dundee* (n.d.), http://internationalwaterlaw.org/bibliography/WWF/RA_European_Union.pdf. (accessed 11 January 2017).

133 According to Salman (n 130), the UNECE Water Convention incorporates detailed provisions on exchange of information and consultation among riparian states "to prevent, control or reduce transboundary impact" of industrialisation on the international waters in the UNECE region.

134 Surya Subedi, 'Regulation of Shared Water Resources in International Law: The Challenge of Balancing Competing Demands' *in* Surya Subedi (ed) *International Watercourse Law for 21st Century: The Case of River Ganges Basin* (Hampshire, Ashgate, 2005) at 18.

135 Alistair Rieu-Clarke et al. (n 132).

136 McCaffrey (n 112).

137 Lipper (n 121) at 15.

claims of co-riparian states and establishing a reasonable balance between conflicting needs.[138]

The equitable and reasonable utilization principle is consistent with the customary international law doctrine of 'limited territorial sovereignty' of states as against extreme positions of 'absolute territorial integrity' and 'absolute territorial sovereignty.' According to Rieu Clarke et al.,

> while the doctrine of absolute territorial sovereignty insists upon the complete freedom of action of the upstream State, the absolute territorial integrity doctrine maintains that the upstream state may do nothing that might affect the natural flow of water into the downstream state.[139]

Vinogradov et al., further explain that 'equitable utilization' is not an "equal portion of the resource or equal share of uses and benefits," but the right of a watercourse state to benefit from the shared water resources and an obligation not to deprive a co-basin state of its own right.[140] This implies that allocation of water resources among co-riparian states is determined by an objective standard judged by the circumstance of each case because it is generally difficult to satisfy all expectations of every riparian state. McIntyre is also of the opinion that the concept of equity in international water law suggests both proportionality and flexibility in sharing the water resources.[141] Furthermore, he observes that under the principle of proportionality, no uses of an international watercourse would be permitted that would result in grossly disproportionate

138 Stephen C. McCaffrey, *The Law of International Watercourses* (2nd edition, Oxford, Oxford University Press, 2007) at 387. According to Rieu-Clarke et al., (n 132) at 12 equitable utilisation principle is "the primary substantive principle of international law relating to transboundary waters allocation."

139 Rieu-Clarke et al. (n 17) at 102. The concept of absolute territorial integrity runs contrary to that of absolute territorial sovereignty. While the former limits the freedom of the upstream state, the latter allows the states to do anything with the watercourse within their territory irrespective of adverse consequences to a co-basin state.

140 S. Vinogradov et al. (n 28) at 17.

141 Owen McIntyre, 'Utilisation (and Environmental Protection) of Shared International Freshwaters: The Role (and Meaning) of Equity." Presentation at the 5th Annual International Water Law and Transboundary Freshwater Workshop, Dundee, 9–13 June 2014. Available at the Centre for Water Law, Policy and Science, University of Dundee.

adverse impacts on other social, developmental, or environmental values and objectives, irrespective of its beneficial purpose.[142]

Both the UN Watercourses Convention and the UNECE Water Convention recognize the principle of equitable and reasonable utilization, but Article 6(1)(a–g) of the UN Watercourses Convention lists the relevant criteria for equitable and reasonable utilization which are not included in the UNECE Water Convention.[143] Article 2(d) of the UNECE Water Convention states the principle generally by recommending that parties should take "all appropriate measures" to use the transboundary waters in an equitable and reasonable way without specifying the relevant factors. In contrast, Article 5 of the UN Watercourses Convention states the principle while Article 6 lists the relevant criteria. Further, Article 6(1) of the UN Watercourses Convention suggests that the list of factors is not exhaustive.[144] Also, none of the factors enjoys priority of weight but "in determination of what is a reasonable and equitable use, all relevant factors are to be considered together and a conclusion reached on the basis of the whole."[145] The only exception is the use of water for vital human needs within the provision of Article 10(2) of the UN Watercourses Convention.[146] According to McIntyre, most of the factors are consistent with sound environmental considerations.[147] Further to this, they are similar

142 Owen McIntyre, 'Utilization of Shared International Freshwater Resources-The Meaning and Role of "Equity" in International Water Law,' *Water International*, Vol. 38, No. 2 (2013), pp. 112–29.

143 The factors are as follows: geographic, hydrographic, hydrological, climatic, ecological and other factors of a natural character; the social and economic needs of the watercourse states concerned; the population dependent on the watercourse in each watercourse state; the effects of the use or uses of the watercourses in one watercourse state on other watercourse states; existing and potential uses of the watercourse; conservation, protection, development and economy of use of the water resources of the watercourse and the costs of measures taken to that effect; and the availability of alternatives, of comparable value, to a particular planned or existing use.

144 Article 6(1) of the UN Watercourses Convention provides that application of the principle of reasonable and equitable utilization must be with consideration of "all relevant factors and circumstances" suggesting factors and circumstances listed and those not listed by the Article.

145 UN Watercourses Convention, art. 6(3).

146 Article 6(3) of the UN Watercourses Convention gives equal weight to all factors for application of the equitable and reasonable utilization principle and Article 10(1) provides that "no use the international watercourse enjoys inherent priority over other uses," but Article 10(2) provides for special consideration to water for "vital human needs."

147 McIntyre observes that "both [the] substantive elements such as the due diligence standards required and ... procedural obligations such as the duty to notify, significantly

to the factors for determination of an "equitable and reasonable share in the beneficial uses of waters of international drainage basin" within Article V(II)(1–11) of the Helsinki Rules.[148] In the Gabčíkovo-Nagymaros Project Case,[149] decided four months after the adoption of the UN Watercourses Convention, the International Court of Justice endorsed the principle of equitable and reasonable utilization together with the relevant factors as principles of customary international law.

2.2.2 Obligation Not to Cause Significant Harm

The principle of equitable and reasonable utilization and the obligation not to cause significant harm or the no harm rule are complementary. However, Tanzi and Arcari note that although more dynamic and use oriented than the prohibition to cause harm, the equitable utilization principle is intended to set more limits to the activities of riparian states on international watercourses.[150]

---

enhances the weight accorded to environmental considerations in the determination of an equitable regime for the utilisation of an international watercourse." Owen McIntyre, 'The Role of Customary Rules and Principles of International Environmental Law in the Protection of Shared International Freshwater Resources,' *Natural Resources Journal*, Vol 46 (2006), pp. 157–210, http://digitalrepository.unm.edu/cgi/viewcontent.cgi?article=1287&context=nrj (accessed 30 August 2017). According to McCaffrey, "the doctrine of equitable utilization does not exist in isolation. It is part of a normative structure that includes procedural requirements necessary for its implementation: the substantive and procedural principles form an integrated whole." McCaffrey (n 36) at 406.

148 According to the Helsinki Rules, the factors are the geography of the basin, including in particular the extent of the drainage area in the territory of each basin state; the hydrology of the basin, including in particular the contribution of water by each basin state; the climate affecting the basin; the past utilization of the waters of the basin, including in particular existing utilization; the economic and social needs of each basin state; the population dependent on the waters of the basin in each basin state; the comparative costs of alternative means of satisfying the economic and social needs of each basin state; the availability of other resources; the avoidance of unnecessary waste in the utilization of waters of the basin; the practicability of compensation to one or more of the co-basin states as a means of adjusting conflicts among uses; and the degree to which the needs of a basin state may be satisfied without causing substantial injury to a co-basin state.

149 The case was brought before the International Court of Justice (ICJ) for resolution of the dispute between Hungary and Slovakia over the Gabčíkovo-Nagymaros Dam project on the Danube River. The ICJ delivered its judgement on 25 September 1997. Available online at http://www.icj-cij.org/files/case-related/92/092-19970925-JUD-01-00-EN.pdf (accessed 30 August 2017).

150 Atilla Tanzi and Maurizio Arcari *The United Nations Convention on the Law of International Watercourses: A Framework for Sharing* (London, Kluwer Law International, 2001) at 147.

They also believe that in the face of conflicting uses the measure of the fair share of water to each state is determined by the equity and reasonableness of their respective uses while the no harm rule is translated to a flexible rule requiring riparian states not to cause harm beyond a minimal threshold which is usually qualified as 'significant' or 'substantial.' McCaffrey observes that the obligation not to cause significant harm does not forbid harm per se but the unreasonable causing of such harm. He further states that the aim is to achieve balance between the conflicting needs of all the party states sharing the international watercourse.[151] Also, according to McIntyre, the prohibition of the no harm rule is not absolute obligation, but is "normally understood to reflect an obligation as to performance, based on standards of due diligence rather than an absolute obligation as to result."[152] The obligation not to cause significant harm, expressed in Latin as *sic utere tuo ut alienum non laedas* (do not use your own as to harm that of another), is also reflected in other UN instruments for protection of the environment.[153] Although both the UN Watercourses Convention and the UNECE Water Convention create an obligation of due diligence to prevent significant transboundary harm, Article 2 of the UNECE Water Convention makes the obligation "to prevent, control and reduce any transboundary impact" mandatory while the provision of the UN Watercourses Convention is more flexible.[154]

2.2.3 Protection of Ecosystems

Both the UN Watercourses Convention and the UNECE Water Convention recognize the obligation to protect the aquatic ecosystems. According to

---

151 McCaffrey (n 138) at 407.

152 McIntyre (n 141). This opinion differentiates due diligence duty of conduct from the duty of result. The due diligence duty of conduct is not an absolute obligation.

153 Article 2 of the Draft Articles on Prevention of Transboundary Harm from Hazardous Activities defines transboundary harm as "harm caused in the territory of or in other places under the jurisdiction or control of a State other than the State of origin, whether or not the States concerned share a common border" while Article 3 states that "the State of origin shall take all appropriate measures to prevent significant transboundary harm or at any event to minimize the risk thereof." This instrument was adopted by the International Law Commission (ILC) in 2001 and is available on line at http://legal.un.org/ilc/texts/instruments/english/commentaries/9_7_2001.pdf. (accessed 26 January 2015). Other UN instruments that reflect this obligation are Principle 21 of 1972 Stockholm Declaration of the United Nations Conference on the Human Environment and Article 3 of the Convention on Biological Diversity.

154 Article 7 of the UN Watercourses Convention calls on states to "take all appropriate measure" to prevent significant harm.

Rieu-Clarke and Kinna, the principle of protection of aquatic ecosystems suggests a link between the right of a riparian state to utilize the water of an international watercourse and an obligation to protect to it.[155] Article 5(1) of the UN Watercourses Convention provides that utilization of the international watercourse must be with regard to interests of the watercourse states consistent with "adequate protection of the watercourse." Also, Article 23 of the Convention states that parties "shall take all measures with respect to an international watercourse ... necessary to protect and preserve the marine environment."[156] Similarly, Article 2(6) of the UNECE Water Convention states that "Riparian Parties shall cooperate to develop ... policies, programmes and strategies covering the relevant catchment areas, ... aimed at the protection of the environment of transboundary waters or the environment influenced by such waters, including the marine environment." Part IV of the UN Watercourses Convention covers ecosystems protection, but the provision of the UNECE Water Convention recognizes some useful environmental principles for protecting the marine environment not included in the UN Watercourses Convention. These are the precautionary principle, the polluter pays principle, and the principle of sustainable development.[157] Furthermore, Article 3 of the UNECE Water Convention defines the types of transboundary pollution that must be prevented, controlled, and reduced and measures to be employed to this end, but Article 21 of the UN Watercourses Convention only encourage parties to arrive at "mutually agreeable measures and methods to prevent, reduce and control pollution of an international watercourse."[158]

155 Rieu-Clarke & Kinna (n 127).

156 The provisions of Article 23 of the UN Watercourses Convention are similar to Article 192 of the United Nations Convention on the Law of the Sea which provides that "States have the obligation to protect and preserve the marine environment." United Nations Convention on the Law of the Sea, 10 December 1982, http://www.un.org/depts/los/convention_agreements/texts/unclos/unclos_e.pdf. (accessed 12 January 2017). A similar provision is found in Chapter 17.22 of Agenda 21, UN Conference on Environment and Development, Rio de Janeiro, 3 to 14 June. https://sustainabledevelopment.un.org/content/documents/Agenda21.pdf (accessed 12 February 2015).

157 UNECE Water Convention, art 2(5). These principles for protection of environment are recognized in the Rio Declaration: Principle 15 (Precautionary Principle), Principle 16 (Polluter Pays Principle), and Principles 3 and 4 (Principle of sustainable Development) Rio Declaration on Environment and Development, June 1992, http://wedocs.unep.org/bitstream/handle/20.500.11822/19163/Rio_Declaration_on_Environment_and_Development.pdf?sequence=1&isAllowed=y. (accessed 30 August 2017).

158 Article 3(2) of the UNECE Water Convention defines the pollution to include both point source and diffuse sources. To control pollution, the Convention mandates party states to

However, Article 22 of the UN Watercourses Convention codifies a ban on introduction of alien or new species, which is not included in the UNECE Water Convention.

2.2.4 The Human Right to Water

Both instruments recognize the principle of the human right to water within a transboundary context. However, while the right to water is recognized within the provision of the UN Watercourses Convention, it is not incorporated in the text of the UNECE Water Convention but in a protocol to the Convention.[159] Article 10 of the UN Watercourses Convention provides that "no use of an international watercourse enjoys inherent priority over other uses" but any conflict of use shall be resolved with regard to water for 'vital human needs.'[160] This provision has been interpreted to mean "sufficient water to sustain human life including both drinking water and water required for production of food in order to prevent starvation."[161] The UNECE Protocol on Water and Health reflects detailed principles of the human right to water and is described as "the first international agreement of its kind adopted specifically to attain an adequate supply of safe drinking water and adequate sanitation for everyone, and effectively protect water used as a source of drinking water."[162] Other UN instruments have also elaborated on the concept of the human right to water[163] and it is also reflected in other water treaties influenced by the provisions of the UN Watercourses Convention.[164]

---

apply low and non-waste technology, license waste water discharges, apply best available technology for discharges of hazardous substances and apply appropriate best environmental practices such as environmental impact assessment and contingency measures. Article 21 of the UN Watercourses Convention encourages parties to set up joint water quality objectives, establish a list of substances to be limited or banned, and develop techniques for addressing point and non-point pollution.

159 UNECE Protocol on Water and Health, London, 17 June 1999. http://www.unece.org/fileadmin/DAM/env/documents/2000/wat/mp.wat.2000.1.e.pdf (accessed 20 January 2017).

160 UN Watercourses Convention, art. 10(2).

161 Vinogradov et al. (n 28) at 23, quoting Statement of Understanding pertaining to the text of Article 10, 1997 UN IWC Convention.

162 'About the Protocol on Water and Health,' *UNECE*. http://www.unece.org/?id=2975 (accessed 15 January 2017).

163 UN Committee on Economic, Social and Cultural Rights, General Comment No. 15: The Right to Water (Arts. 11 and 12 of the Covenant),' 20 January 2003, E/C. 12/2002/11, http://www.refworld.org/docid/4538838d11.html (accessed 15 January 2017).

164 The Human right to water is included in Article 4 of the Niger Basin Water Charter and Article 4(3)(b) of the SADC Water Protocol. Protocol on Shared Watercourses in

2.3 *Procedural Rules*

Article 9 of the UN Watercourses Convention codifies the obligation of parties to cooperate for "optimal utilization and adequate protection of the international watercourse." The need for cooperation in the management of transboundary water is also stated in Article 2(6) of the UNECE Water Convention and was discussed in the Lac Lanoux Arbitration Case.[165] The obligation of the parties to cooperate as codified in the UN Watercourses Convention is more direct than the provision of cooperation in the UNECE Water Convention. The UNECE Water Convention emphasizes institutional cooperation through agreements and joint programs rather than providing statement on the obligation to cooperate.

Articles 11 to 19 of the UN Watercourses Convention codify elaborate provisions on the principle of prior notification of planned measures and give details on this obligation. The obligation includes notification to a co-riparian state that could be significantly and negatively affected by the measure; the notification must be timely; and the notified states could begin a process of consultations and, if necessary commence negotiation for equitable resolution if it believes the proposed project or measure is inconsistent with Article 5 or 7 of the Convention.[166] Article 9 of the UNECE Water Convention provides forms of notification such as exchange of data, joint monitoring programs on water quality, prior licensing and monitoring of wastewater discharges, warning and alarm procedures, and exchange of information on existing and planned uses of water and related installations that are likely to have a

---

the Southern African Development Community (SADC Water Protocol) was adopted in Windhoek, 7 August 2000 and entered in force in 22 September 2003. http://www.internationalwaterlaw.org/documents/regionaldocs/Revised-SADC-SharedWatercourse-Protocol-2000.pdf (accessed 15 January 2017).

165 The Lac Lanoux arbitration between French and Spain concerned the use of the waters of Lac Lanoux and was decided on 16 November 1957. According to the Arbitral Tribunal, "States are today perfectly conscious of the importance of the conflicting interests brought into play by the industrial use of international rivers, and of the necessity to reconcile them by mutual concessions. The only way to arrive at such compromises of interests is to conclude agreements on an increasingly comprehensive basis ... There would thus appear to be an obligation to accept in good faith all communications and contacts which could, by a broad comparison of interests and by reciprocal good will, provide States with the best conditions for concluding agreements". Lake Lanoux Arbitration (France v. Spain), (1957) 12 R.I.A.A. 281; 24 I.L.R. 101. http://www.ecolex.org/server2.php/libcat/docs/COU/Full/En/COU-143747E.pdf (accessed 26 January 2017).

166 Article 5 of the UN Watercourses Convention sets out the equitable and reasonable utilization principle while Article 7 codifies the obligation not to cause significant harm.

transboundary impact. Although these are not recognized in detail in the UN Watercourses Convention, the UNECE Water Convention fails to define the process of notification, which is set out in the UN Watercourses Convention.

On exchange of data and information among riparian states, Article 13(1) of the UNECE Water Convention not only makes it mandatory, but provides the types of relevant data parties must exchange.[167] Article 9 the UN Watercourses Convention encourages party states to exchange data and information but this is subject to Article 31 which provides that information could be withheld when it is "vital to national defence and security" of the watercourse state. In the contrast, Article 8 of the UNECE Water Convention allows party states to withhold "information related to industrial and commercial secrecy, including intellectual property or national security." According to Tanzi, a major difference between the two treaties is that the UN Watercourses Convention excludes the right to withhold commercial or industrial information that is deemed confidential while the UNECE Water Convention protects it. However, neither convention covers a wide scope of exemptions to the release of information such as is envisaged by the Aarhus Convention on Access to Information, Public Participation in Decision-making and Access to Justice in Environmental Matters.[168]

---

167 The data must relate to environmental conditions of transboundary waters; experience gained in the application and operation of best available technology and results of research and development; emission and monitoring; measures taken and planned to be taken to prevent, control and reduce transboundary impact; or permits or regulations for wastewater discharges issued by the competent authority or appropriate body.

168 The UNECE adopted the Aarhus Convention on 25 June 1998, http://www.unece.org/fileadmin/DAM/env/pp/documents/cep43e.pdf (accessed 15 January 2017). Article 4(4) of the Aarhus Convention provides that a request for environmental information may be refused if the disclosure would adversely affect the confidentiality of the proceedings of public authorities, where such confidentiality is provided for under national law; international relations, national defence or public security; the course of justice or the ability of a person to receive a fair trial or the ability of a public authority to conduct an enquiry of a criminal disciplinary nature; the confidentiality of commercial and industrial information where such confidentiality is protected by law in order to protect a legitimate economic interest; intellectual property rights; the confidentiality of personal data and/or files relating to natural person where that person has not consented to the disclosure of the information to the public, where such confidentiality is provided for in national law; the interests of a third party which has supplied the information requested without that party being under or capable of being put under a legal obligation to do so, and where that party does not consent to the release of the material; or the environment to which the information relates, such as the breeding sites of rare species.

2.4 *Institutional Framework*

While the UNECE Water Convention is more detailed and instructive, emphasizing institutional cooperation through treaties or agreement, joint programs, and joint bodies, the UN Watercourses Convention only encourages parties to have institutions.[169] According to McCaffrey

> the management of international watercourse systems through joint institutions is ... a form of cooperation between watercourse States that is indispensable if anything approaching optimum utilisation of the system of waters is to be attained.[170]

Unlike the UNECE Water Convention, the UN Watercourses Convention lacks a formal structure or institutional framework to implement co-operation. It also lacks mandatory provisions for riparian states to have basin agreements and joint basin commissions. Rather, Article 8(2) of the UN Watercourses Convention creates a flexible position that "States may consider the establishment of joint mechanisms or commission." In contrast, Article 9(1) of the UNECE Water Convention mandates that

> the Riparian Parties shall on the basis of equality and reciprocity enter into bilateral or multilateral agreements or other arrangements, where these do not yet exist or adapt existing ones, where necessary to eliminate the contradictions with the basic principles of this Convention.

Article 24(1) of the UN Watercourses Convention, which states that "Watercourse States shall, at the request of any of them, enter into consultations concerning the management of an international watercourse, which may include the establishment of a joint management mechanism," is also very flexible. Article 17 of the UNECE Water Convention creates the 'Meeting of Parties' as the key institution for cooperation and implementation of the Convention but this is absent in the UN Watercourses Convention.

---

169 Article 2(6) of the UNECE Water Convention states that "Riparian States shall cooperate on the basis of equality and reciprocity, in particular through bilateral and multilateral agreements ..." The Preamble to the Convention recognizes that "cooperation between member countries in regard to the protection and use of transboundary waters shall be implemented primarily through the elaboration of agreements between countries bordering the same waters, especially where no such agreements have yet been reached."

170 Rieu-Clarke et al. (n 17) at 191–92, quoting Stephen McCaffrey (Special Rapporteur), *ILC Sixth Report on the Law of the Non-navigational Uses of International Watercourses*.

As observed, the UN Watercourses Convention "lacks provisions on governance mechanisms and there is nobody mandated to oversee its implementation."[171] Consistent with this opinion, the need for an institutional body not properly conceived within the framework of implementing the provisions of the UN Watercourses Convention has recently come into the limelight. In order to harmonize activities under both the UN Watercourses Convention and the UNECE Water Convention, a discussion paper presented by Kinna, Rieu-Clarke and Loures offers three options for an institutional framework.[172] First there is the 'combined option approach' which suggests creating a formal institution framework for the UN Watercourses Convention with the UNECE Water Convention secretariat servicing both conventions. Second, the 'parallel option approach' suggests that a formal institutional framework for both conventions distinct from each other be created. Third, the 'status quo option' implies that "no formal institutional framework for the UN Watercourses Convention is created following its entry into force." Under the final option, Kinna, Rieu-Clarke and Loures suggest that in the meantime parties to the UN Watercourses Convention could use informal institutions for operation without necessarily amending the treaty.

2.5 *Dispute Resolution Mechanisms*

Article 33 of the UN Watercourses Convention and the annex titled 'Arbitration' create a detailed procedure for dispute settlement. Accordingly, the process should start with negotiations between the parties, which could then proceed to good offices, mediation, or conciliation by a third party. The parties could also agree to submit the dispute to a joint watercourse institution established by them or to the International Court of Arbitration. The dispute could also be submitted to an impartial fact-finding commission after six months of negotiation. In contrast, Article 22 of the UNECE Water Convention only establishes two means of dispute resolution namely, submission of a dispute to the International Court of Justice or arbitration.'[173] According to Tanzi,

171 Remy Kinna, Alistair Rieu-Clarke & Flavia Loures 'Global UN Water Conventions: Options for Coordinated Implementation' at 1, http://www.unwatercoursesconvention.org/documents/discussion-paper-global-un-water-conventions-options-for-coordinated-implementation.pdf (accessed 17 September 2017).

172 Ibid. at 2–5.

173 UNECE Water Convention, art. 22(2)(a) and (b).

> the absence of any express provisions in art. 22 of the UNECE Water Convention to other forms of dispute settlement, such as good-offices, enquiry, mediation or conciliation, and the lack of, even encouragement to refer the dispute to joint watercourse institutions as- in art. 33, para. 2 of the [UN Watercourses Convention]—should be appreciated against the background of the obligation under the [UNECE Water Convention] to establish joint bodies for bilateral and multilateral co-operation, whose tasks under arts. 9 *et seq* cover the widest range of prevention and joint management measures that have a direct impact on dispute avoidance.[174]

Nonetheless, the UNECE Water Convention has very limited dispute resolution mechanisms and processes compared to Article 33 of the UN Watercourses Convention.

2.6 *Contrasting the UN Watercourses Convention and the UNECE Water Convention*

The UN Watercourses Convention is often seen as a codification of the customary international water law. Elaborate provisions made by the Convention of the principles of equitable and reasonable utilization and also prevention of significant harm (substantive) and prior notification of planned measures (procedural) are particularly significant. Although the Convention received widespread recognition and acceptance from the floor of the adoption at the United Nations General Assembly, it suffered from a slow ratification process by many states including the ones that voted for its adoption. As a result, it did not enter into force until more than a decade after its adoption.[175] Meanwhile the UNECE Water Convention entered into force shortly after its adoption, and the amendment to the Convention that permits non-UNECE states to become contracting parties has recently entered into force.

Given that the UNECE Convention started as a regional instrument while the UN Watercourses Convention was adopted as global instrument, it could be assumed that the 'globalization' of the UNECE Water Convention will generate conflict when principles of both treaties are simultaneously implemented in same region. However, Kinna and Rieu-Clarke suggest that the UN Watercourses Convention and the UNECE Water Convention "are not mutually exclusive but

174 Tanzi (n 129) at 39.

175 On 21 May 2014, the thirty-fifth nation, Vietnam acceded to the UN Watercourses Convention and in compliance with Article 36 (1), the Convention entered into force the ninetieth day following this ratification or accession, which was 17 August 2014.

in several ways complement each other and that key differences between the two instruments relate to context rather than content."[176] Whatever position is taken, it is pertinent to note that although both UN water treaties focus on achieving the same goal of cooperative management of shared watercourses, they were set out as different instruments and should operate independently while still benefitting from each other's strengths and learning from each other's weaknesses. The UN Watercourses Convention is more flexible in many respects than the UNECE Water Convention. The flexibility is consistent with the reasoning that a

> treaty regime as a whole need not and should not be held to a standard of strict compliance but to a level of overall compliance that is 'acceptable' in the light of the interests and concerns the treaty is designed to safeguard.[177]

As a framework treaty designed to be global *ab initio*, the UN Watercourses Convention encourages different interpretations and application of its provisions by states.

Wouters and Vinogradov conclude that "both instruments are significantly different"[178] but it has also been observed that in the differences, they are "mutually reinforcing"[179] Since the UNECE Water Convention is older (in operation, about two decades) while the UN Watercourses Convention has just entered into force, contracting states implementing the UN Watercourses Convention can definitely learn from the projects, programs and institutional framework of the UNECE Water Convention. Consistently, states in the same region could "capitalize on the global legitimacy of the UNWC and the 20 years of experience under the UNECE Water Convention towards progressively building a legally mandated, effective and truly global transboundary water regime."[180] Both UN Water treaties are framework conventions that influenced the post-1990 water regimes in West Africa. Can accession to both regimes by West African states add value to transboundary water management and cooperation in the region?

176 Rieu-Clarke & Kinna (n 127) at 15.

177 Abram Chayes and Antonia Handler Chayes, 'On Compliance,' *International Organization*, Vol. 47, No. 2 (Spring 1993), pp. 175–205 at 176.

178 Patricia Wouters and Sergei Vinogradov (n 131).

179 Remy Kinna et al., (n 171) at 1.

180 Ibid. at 2.

3.0 Current Transboundary Treaty Architecture in West Africa (Post 1990)

Although the Economic Community of West African States (ECOWAS) has developed regional water resources policy for member states, the policy is currently a non-binding soft law.[181] Current transboundary water resources management and co-operation in West Africa is at different levels within the West Africa's river basins. Riparian states of the six major transboundary watercourses in West Africa have adopted treaties or agreements for cooperation and management of their shared watercourses. Following adoption of the UN Watercourses Convention and the UNECE Water Convention in the 1990s, texts of the treaties adopted thereafter are inspired by the two UN water treaties, particularly the UN Watercourses Convention. Not only do preambles to most treaties adopted in the region in this era recognize the importance of these UN water treaties, the regimes also reflect the five elements of shared watercourse instruments recognised under international water law.[182] Some of the regimes codify emerging principles of shared watercourse management such as the human right to water, minimum streamflow, public participation, integrated basin management and common works; principles that are not necessarily reflected in the UN water treaties.[183] Water regimes signed in West Africa following adoption of the UN water treaties are the Niger Basin Water Charter; the

181 In 2007 and 2008 ECOWAS states adopted the soft laws, Regional Water Policy and ECOWAS West Africa Water Resources Policy respectively. According to 'USLegal,' soft law means "rules that are neither strictly binding in nature nor completely lacking legal significance. In the context of international law, soft law refers to guidelines, policy declarations or codes of conduct which set standards of conduct. However, they are not directly enforceable". See 'Soft Law and Legal Definition,' *USlegal*. http://definitions.uslegal.com/s/soft-law/. (accessed 1 February 2017).

182 The five elements are scope, substantive provisions, procedural provisions, institutional framework, and the dispute resolution provisions. the substantive obligations are the principle of equitable and reasonable utilization; the obligation not to cause significant harm (or no harm rule) and protection of ecosystems, while the procedural principles are obligation to cooperate, notification of planned measures, and exchange of data and information.

183 Although article 10 of the UN Watercourses Convention recognizes the importance of water for vital human needs, the instrument lacks provisions on minimum streamflow, public participation and common works. Similarly, the Protocol on Water and Health under the UNECE Water Convention addresses the human right to water but no provision was made for minimum streamflow, public participation and common works.

Charter of Waters of the Senegal River (Senegal River Water Charter);[184] the Water Charter for the Lake Chad Basin (Lake Chad Basin Water Charter); the Convention on the Status of the Volta River and Establishment of the Volta Basin Authority (Volta River Basin Convention), and the Code of Conduct for Sustainable and Equitable Management of Shared Water Resources of the Volta Basin (Volta Basin Code of Conduct) which is soft law. The Gambia River Basin states have not contracted any treaty since the 1978 Gambia River Basin Convention, but the Gambia River Basin Development Organisation is currently working towards a new water charter.[185]

Though the West African modern transboundary water agreements are influenced by the UN water treaties, they do not present a consistent pattern. These instruments could be grouped into two categories. The first category is those instruments that are clearly influenced by the provisions of the UN Watercourses Convention and the UNECE Water Convention, such as the Niger Basin Water Charter, the Lake Chad Basin Water Charter, and the Volta Basin Code of Conduct between Ghana and Burkina Faso. The second category comprises instruments that show limited influence by the UN water treaties and includes the Senegal River Water Charter and the Volta River Basin Convention. In this second category, the Senegal River Water Charter is an improvement of the old Convention Relating to the Status of the River Senegal regarding principles of transboundary water resources management. Some of these instruments recognize emerging principles of the human right to water, public participation and common works better than the UN water regimes.[186]

3.1 *Approaches to the Scope of Modern West African Transboundary Water Instruments*

There are three key trends in the scope of the current West Africa water regimes. The first trend is evident in the Lake Chad Basin Water Charter, the only instrument that comprehensively and directly covers both surface water and groundwater of the basin. Article 1 defines the scope of the Lake Chad

184 The Charter of Waters of the Senegal River was adopted in May, 2002. http://iea.uoregon.edu/pages/view_treaty.php?t=2002-senegalriverwatercharter.en.txt&par=view_treaty_html (accessed 16 January 2017).

185 See OMVG (n 90).

186 Article 2 of the Senegal River Water Charter, Chapter VII of the Niger Basin Water Charter, Article 203, para 3 and 4 of the Appendix to Niger Basin Water Charter, Article 15 of the Volta Basin Code of Conduct, and Article 78 of Lake Chad Basin Water Charter recognize the principle of public participation.

international waters as "the watercourses, aquifers and aquatic ecosystem."[187] This is similar to the scope of the UNECE Water Convention and wider than that of the UN Watercourses Convention, which excludes confined aquifers.[188]

The second trend is the ambiguous position set out in the Volta River Basin Convention and the Niger Basin Water Charter. These instruments state that they are applicable only to surface water, but later in the document give power over groundwater to relevant authorities.[189] Similarly, ambiguous provisions in Article 4 of the Volta Basin Code of Conduct state that the instrument applies to 'shared water resources' of the river basin without defining the extent of the shared water resources and whether it is groundwater inclusive. The implication is that the scope as defined by these instruments is not as direct as the scope of both UN water regimes. The third trend found in the Senegal River Water Charter restricts the scope of the treaty to surface water. Article 1 of the Charter defines the catchment area of the Senegal River as the "River Senegal, its effluents, distributaries and associated depressions" which excludes the groundwater and partially conforms to the scope of the UN water treaties.[190]

Unlike the UN Watercourses Convention, all the West African water treaties are applicable for different uses of the transboundary watercourses, including navigation.[191] Although application of the treaties to navigation is becoming less common, in West Africa navigation is still relevant because people living close to the banks of transboundary watercourses are mainly rural dwellers

187 Aquifer in this context includes both confined and fossil aquifers in the Lake Chad Basin. Clearly the instrument applies to both the surface water, referred to as "the watercourses" and the ground water (aquifers).

188 Article 1 of the Fort Lamy Convention (n 83) defines the Chad Basin as "the area delimited by the map appended to the Convention" referring to surface water only.

189 The Volta River Basin Convention defines the 'international river' as the Volta River, its tributaries and sub tributaries, but Article 7, which states that the functions of the Volta Basin Authority extend its jurisdiction over Volta River, its tributaries, sub-tributaries, lakes, wetlands and groundwater linked to the Basin. Similarly, Article 3 of the Niger Basin Water Charter describes the scope of the Charter as the Niger River, its tributaries, sub-tributaries and distributaries but Article 11 of the Charter authorizes state parties to "develop and implement planning, protection, management, use and development policies for groundwater and surface water." It is unclear if the groundwater is merely connected to the surface water or both confined and unconfined aquifer.

190 Both the UN Watercourses Convention and the UNECE Water Convention apply to surface water and groundwater although the UNECE Water Convention covers confined and unconfined groundwater while the UN Watercourses Convention is limited to unconfined groundwater.

191 The UNECE Water Convention is silent on 'navigation' but it could be argued that the scope encompasses it.

who engage in subsistence farming, fishing and trading and use the watercourses for transportation in support of these activities. However, the provisions on navigation in these current regimes are not as comprehensive as in earlier treaties.[192]

3.2 *Substantive Norms in Modern West African Transboundary Water Treaties*

Like the UN Watercourses Convention and the UNECE Water Convention, current water regimes in West Africa recognize obligations. They offer a package approach to the substantive norms, incorporating equitable and reasonable utilization, no significant harm, protection of ecosystems, and the human right to water, but the degree of recognition varies between regimes.

3.2.1 Reasonable and Equitable Utilization

The principle of equitable and reasonable utilization of the shared watercourses is codified in all of the West African water regimes under consideration. While some of them reflect the principle extensively, as in the UN Watercourses Convention, others briefly state it, as is the case in the UNECE Water Convention. Closest to the first approach are the Niger Basin Water Charter and the Lake Chad Basin Water Charter. Article 4 of the Niger Basin Water Charter incorporates the principle of equitable and reasonable utilization and also includes the relevant factors. Article 10 of the Lake Chad Basin Water Charter codifies the principle, while Article 13 lists the relevant criteria. The factors listed in both treaties are compatible with the factors listed in Article 6 of UN Watercourses Convention, though they are more than the seven factors listed in the Convention.[193] Article 6 of the UN Watercourses Convention encourages consideration of other 'relevant factors and circumstances' for reasonable and equitable utilization of international watercourses. Similarly, Article 12 of the Lake Chad Basin Water Charter states that "State parties may agree to determine other relevant factors to be taken into account

192 Article 14 of the Niger Basin Water Charter lists navigation as one of the recognized uses of the River but the Act of Niamey dedicated Articles 2 and 3 to navigation. Similarly the whole of Part III comprising five articles of the Gambia River Basin Convention deals with navigation.

193 Article 4 of the Niger Basin Water Charter lists fifteen factors, including the "existence of minimum environmental flow to be preserved so as to maintain the services of the River Niger Basin and the Wetlands" while Article 12 of the Lake Chad Basin Water Charter lists eighteen factors and adds a provision that "State parties may agree to determine other relevant factors to be taken into account considering local circumstances and the various needs of water."

considering local circumstances and the various needs of water." The implication is that the relevant factors for determining the equitable utilization principle are inexhaustible and some social and environmental considerations generate more factors.[194] According to McIntyre, among the relevant factors

> considerations relating to environmental protection of international watercourses are steadily increasing due to the emergence of a comprehensive set of rules, principles, and legal concepts requiring enhanced protection of various aspects of the natural environment of international watercourses and riparian States.[195]

Both the Niger Basin Water Charter and the Lake Chad Basin Water Charter are obviously influenced by the UN Watercourses Convention in their elaborate provision of the principle of equitable and reasonable utilization.

The second trend concerning recognition of the principle of reasonable and equitable utilization in West Africa water regimes is found in the Senegal River Water Charter, the Volta Basin Code of Conduct, and the Volta River Basin Convention. These instruments state the principle very briefly thereby demonstrating the minimal influence of the UN Watercourses Convention.[196] The equitable utilization principle in these treaties resembles that of the UNECE Water Convention where it is briefly set out within the 'General Provisions.'[197] The Niger Basin Water Charter and the Lake Chad Basin Water Charter dedicate a separate article to the equitable utilization principle and a further to

194 Some of the environmental factors dealing with the equitable and reasonable utilization principle in the Niger Basin Water Charter are the need to avoid waste in the use of the Basin waters, preservation of minimum environmental flow, sharing of water resources between all users, aquatic systems and associated ecosystems; the Lake Chad Basin instrument deals with ecosystem requirements in the wetlands, maintenance of minimum streamflow, the cumulative effect of abstractions and pollution on the watercourse, aquifer and aquatic ecosystems, the need for conservation, protection, development and careful use of the water resources of the Basin, and the effect of climate variability and climate change.

195 McIntyre (n 147) at 159.

196 Article 4 of the Volta River Basin Convention includes the equitable utilization principle as one of the guides for cooperation and sustainability of the water resources; Article 4 of the Charter of Waters of the Senegal River states that the principle of equitable and reasonable use of the water is one of the determinants to guide distribution of water among uses. Both of the instruments fail to list factors that deal with reasonable and equitable utilization and measures for mitigating harm.

197 UNECE Water Convention, art. 2(2)(c).

the guiding factors. The Volta Basin Code of Conduct defines the "principle of equitable use" in a distinct article, but it is briefly stated without relevant factors.[198]

3.2.2 Obligation Not to Cause Significant Harm

The Lake Chad Basin Water Charter is the only regime that states the no harm rule obligation as set out in the UN Watercourses Convention. According to McCaffrey, the no harm rule obligation does not prohibit the causing of significant harm *per se* but rather the unreasonable causing of such harm.[199] Like Article 7 of the UN Watercourses Convention, which sets the standard of 'substantial harm' and places the obligation as that of due diligence duty of conduct and not duty of result, Article 42 of the Lake Chad Basin Water Charter obliges parties to take measures "to prevent significant harm" thereby linking the obligation to the principle of reasonable and equitable utilization. The Lake Chad regime also recommends measures for preventing and mitigating transboundary harm that are similar to measures for preventing transboundary impact as set out in Article 4 of the UNECE Water Convention.[200]

The cursory codification of the no harm rule obligation in the Niger Basin Water Charter is not consistent with the provisions of the UN Watercourses Convention.[201] Article 5 of the Water Charter states that "parties shall see to the fact that the activities conducted in their territories do not cause harm to other state parties …" Here, the statement of the obligation is not only brief, but is also not linked to the equitable and reasonable utilization principle. Like the Niger Basin Water Charter, the Volta River Basin Convention also briefly codifies the no harm rule obligation, but not in a separate article as in the Niger Basin Water Charter. The no harm rule obligation in the Volta River Basin Convention is recognized as one of the principles for rational and sustainable utilization of the water resources of the Volta River Basin under Article 4.[202] While the Volta Basin Code of Conduct states the 'no harm rule'

198 Volta Basin Code of Conduct, art. 11.

199 McCaffrey (n 112).

200 Article 44 to 48 of the Lake Chad Basin Water Charter defines the measures as consultation, no discrimination when remedying damage, environmental impact assessment, environmental audits, and strategic environmental assessment.

201 Article 5 of the Niger Basin Water Charter sets out the no harm rule very briefly without providing mitigation measures but Article 7 of the UN Watercourses Convention not only creates an obligation on state parties not to cause significant harm but also further an obligation to take "appropriate measures" to mitigate any harm caused.

202 Other principles listed in the article are equitable and reasonable use of water, regular exchange of data, notification on planned activities, precaution and prevention, protection

obligation indirectly; the Senegal River Water Charter lacks any statement of the no harm rule obligation.[203]

3.2.3 Protection of Ecosystems

Like the substantive principles discussed above, the principle of protection of ecosystems is reflected in all of the water regimes in West Africa but in one of two ways. Hence, there are instruments that show the profound inspiration of the UN water treaties and those that state the principle briefly. The provision for protection of ecosystems in the Niger Basin Water Charter and the Lake Chad Basin Water Charter are influenced by both UN water treaties, particularly with respect to pollution control. Both instruments list measures for pollution control similar to the provisions of the UN Watercourses Convention.[204] In the UN Watercourses Convention, 'protection of ecosystems' includes instruction to party states to prevent introduction of alien or new species[205] and to prevent or mitigate hazard.[206] The Niger Basin Water Charter and the Lake Chad Basin Water Charter direct riparian states to "control invasive aquatic species," which is a bit looser than the UN Watercourses Convention provision of 'prevention' of invasion of alien species.[207] Like the UN Watercourses Convention, the Lake Chad Basin Water Charter defines the natural disasters and also

---

and conservation of ecosystems, notification of emergency situation and freedom of navigation on the river.

203 Article 12 of the Volta Basin Code of Conduct, Pollution Prevention and Polluter Pays Principle, states that "states shall take all necessary measures to prevent, stop or minimize any possible pollution factors which may endanger people, the environment, and the water resources of the Basin" and indirectly creates the no harm rule obligation.

204 Article 12 of Niger Basin Water Charter provides for protection and preservation of the environment and also lists measures such as protection of wetlands, promotion of sustainable use of water, protection of the aquatic environment, reduction of transboundary pollution, systematic environmental assessments; development and management of the catchment area, preservation of biodiversity of the catchment area and prevention of siltation. Similarly, Section 2 of Lake Chad Basin Water Charter, "Conservation of Biological Diversity" has five articles on the protection of the Basin's ecosystem through protection of aquatic ecosystem (Article 28), prevention of environmental damage (Article 29), control of invasive aquatic species (Article 30), prevention of soil degradation (Article 31), and rehabilitation and management of the Basin's vegetation cover (Article 32).

205 UN Watercourses Convention, art 22.

206 Article 27 of the UN Watercourses Convention defines the hazard as "flood or ice conditions, waterborne diseases, siltation, erosion, salt water intrusion, drought or desertification."

207 Niger Basin Water Charter, art. 12 and Lake Chad Basin Water Charter, art. 30. 'Control' is wider than 'prevent' and could mean permit some invasion of alien species.

elaborates contingency plans for their prevention and control.[208] Article 3(1)(j) of the UNECE Water Convention only provides that parties should take 'appropriate measures' to control and reduce transboundary impacts, including contingency planning without defining the disasters.

Unlike the Niger Basin Water Charter and the Lake Chad Basin Water Charter, statements concerning the principle of protection of ecosystems or the environment of shared watercourses in the other instruments are very brief. Apart from the Volta Basin Code of Conduct, no instrument presents the obligation as a separate provision.[209] Article 4 of the Volta River Basin Convention includes protection and conservation of ecosystems as one of the principles of commitment of the state parties for cooperation and sustainable utilization of water resources of the Volta River Basin. However, the measures for protecting the environment are not appropriately defined. Similarly, Article 4 of the Senegal River Water Charter creates the "obligation to preserve the environment" as one of the principles to guide distribution of water between uses.[210]

3.3 *Procedural Norms in Modern West African Transboundary Water Treaties*

Almost all of the current shared watercourses regimes in West Africa agree on some procedural obligations like cooperation, prior notification of planned measures, consultation, and the exchange of data. Generally, the instruments can be classified into two categories: those aligned to the UN Watercourses Convention and UNECE Water Convention such as the Niger Basin Water Charter, the Lake Chad Basin Water Charter, and the Volta River Basin Code of Conduct and those instruments that codified the provisions of the UN water treaties superficially, such as the Senegal River Water Charter and the Volta River Basin Convention.

---

208 Articles 37 to 41 of the Lake Chad Basin Water Charter provide measures for managing disasters, which are defined as flood and drought.

209 Article 30 of the Volta Basin Code of Conduct, "Principle of priority conservation of aquatic ecosystems" states the provision and also the implication of protecting the ecosystem of the river basin to include "regulation and renewal of water resources and to its social, economic and cultural dimension." This benefit is not reflected in any water treaty provision in West Africa.

210 Article 5 of the Senegal River water Charter provides that integrated management of the water resources should take into account the availability and continuity of the resource, "integration of the dimension of the environment in the management of water and the durable maintenance of the favourable conditions in the basin of the River," and provisions relating to protection of ecosystem, which are linked to other considerations for integrated management of the water resources like permanent navigability of the river.

3.3.1 Obligation to Cooperate

Garane observes that transboundary water agreements and institutions in West Africa are established to "ensure cooperation for control, management and protection of the international watercourse."[211] According to Leb, "experience in transboundary basins shows that cooperation among riparian States more often leads to greater benefits for all basin States than non-cooperation" because cooperation in management of shared watercourses resolves all competing interests in the basin.[212] Furthermore, it overlaps with other principles and rules of international law and brings them to fruition. Principles of equitable and reasonable utilization, the no harm rule, notification of planned measures, and good neighborliness "cannot be adequately implemented without cooperation."[213] Leb further argues that general duty to cooperate "serves as a bridge between substantive and procedural rules."[214] Like the initial instruments adopted for management of share watercourses in West Africa, current regimes are founded on the desire of the states to cooperate. In most of the treaties this obligation is inferred from other provisions within the instrument that emphasize institutional cooperation but without a direct statement of an obligation to cooperate.[215]

The Lake Chad Basin Water Charter directly codifies the principle of obligation to cooperate in a manner similar to Article 8 of the UN Watercourses Convention, but with a proviso that "Parties shall cooperate within the [Lake Chad Basin] Commission."[216] The Niger Basin Water Charter defines the

211 Garane (n 69) at 97. Chapter 18. 4 of Agenda 21 (n 56) provides that "transboundary water resources and their use are of great importance to riparian States. In this connection, cooperation among those States may be desirable in conformity with existing agreements and/or other relevant arrangements, taking into account the interests of all riparian States concerned."

212 Leb (n 33) at 1.

213 Ibid. at 4.

214 Ibid. at 110.

215 Article 2 of the Niger Basin Water Charter encourages "cooperation based on solidarity and reciprocity" and also reflects elements of cooperation in several other provisions within the treaty even though the treaty lacks direct recognition of the obligation to cooperate. Institutional cooperation through the river basin organizations (RBOs) is encouraged by Article 9 of the UNECE Water Convention.

216 Article 8 of the Lake Chad Basin Water Charter creates a "general obligation to cooperate." Cooperation must be within the supervision of the Lake Chad Basin Commission. Article 7 of the Water Charter also provides that implementation of the instrument shall be guided by principles of sustainable development, information and participation, precaution, solidarity, cooperation, and partnership among others.

purpose of the Charter, which is "to encourage cooperation based on solidarity and reciprocity for a sustainable, equitable and coordinated use" of the Niger River Basin.[217] Although the instrument lacks any statement of an obligation to cooperate, cooperation flows from the purpose of the Charter to the principle of 'shared vision,' which was adopted by the Niger Basin Authority. Similarly, Article 4 of Senegal River Water Charter reflects the principle of cooperation through other principles that guide distribution of water resources.[218] The Volta Basin Code of Conduct and the Volta River Basin Convention include a brief indirect statement of the obligation to cooperate.[219]

3.3.2 Notification of Planned Measures

The principle of notification of any planned project in the basin and exchange of information features in the post-colonial shared watercourse regimes in West Africa as the main reason for cooperation.[220] The rationale is that unregulated projects and measures in the shared watercourse could adversely affect other riparian states and the integrity of the river basin. The Gambia River Basin Convention took the lead in providing a time frame for notification that was subsequently adopted by most current West Africa water treaties.[221] Though these regimes have detailed provisions concerning notification on planned measures or projects and exchange of data/information, their approach is not similar. The first trend is that of a comprehensive straightforward procedure of notification similar to Part III, (Articles 11 to 19) of the UN Watercourses Convention. This is the case with the Niger Basin Water Charter, the Lake Chad Basin Water Charter, and the Senegal River Water Charter. Unlike the UN Watercourses Convention, these treaties provide

217 Niger Basin Water Charter, art. 2.

218 Article 4 of the Senegal River Water Charter states that "distribution of water between the uses is in particular founded on the following general principles: obligation to guarantee the balanced management of the water resource; the equitable and reasonable use of water of the River; obligation to preserve the environment; obligation to negotiate in the event of conflict; and the obligation for each coastal state to inform the other coastal states before undertaking any action or any project which could have an impact on the availability of water and/or the possibility of implementing future projects.

219 Volta Basin Code of Conduct, art. 10; Volta River Basin Convention, art. 4.

220 Act of Niamey, arts 4 and 5; 1964 NRC Agreement, art. 12; Fort Lamy Convention, art. 5.

221 Article 4 of the Gambia River Basin Convention provides for a notification period of six months, similar to Article 13 of the UN Watercourses Convention but does not state that it must be done through the OMVG.

for notification through the executive secretariat of the river basin organizations (RBOs) recognized by Article 9(2)(h) of the UNECE Water Convention.[222]

Article 19 of the Niger Basin Water Charter defines the obligation to exchange information, engage in consultations, and negotiate on possible effects of planned measures while Article 20 provides guidelines for notification.[223] Chapter 8 of the Lake Chad Basin Water Charter has the same provision, but it provides for a four-month notification period; the UN Watercourses Convention and the Niger Basin Water Charter provide for a six-month and three-month notification period respectively. The provision in the Niger Basin Water Charter on the effect of non-reply to notification is similar to that of Article 16 of the UN Watercourses Convention, but different from Article 56 the Lake Chad Basin Water Charter. While both the UN Watercourses Convention and the Niger Basin Water Charter allow the notifying party to proceed with the project at the expiration of the period of notification, Article 56 of the Lake Chad Basin Water Charter provides for further examination of the planned measure by a special body if the state parties affected by the measure fails to respond within a time frame of four months.[224] As provided for under Article 19 of the UN Watercourses Convention, both the Niger Basin Water Charter and the Lake Chad Basin Water Charter offer an exemption for the notification period when implementation of the planned measure is urgently needed for public health and safety.[225] Article 4 of the Senegal River Water Charter creates an obligation to inform all other riparian states of any planned project and,

---

222 Articles 12 and 23 of the UN Watercourses Convention suggest direct notification of the affected states, while Article 9(2)(h) of the UNECE Water Convention mandates parties to establish joint bodies in bilateral or multilateral agreements "to serve as forum for exchange of information on existing and planned uses of water and related installations that are likely to cause transboundary impact."

223 Article 20 of the Niger Basin Water Charter provides that a measure must be deemed to have a significant adverse effect on other Basin States, notification must be timely, notification must be through the Executive Secretariat, and the notification must be accompanied by relevant data, including social and environmental impact assessment of the measure.

224 Article 56 of the Lake Chad Basin Water Charter provides for examination of the measure by the Water Resources Advisory Committee and the Environment, Science and Planning Advisory Committee. The Niger Basin Water Charter allows the notifying state to proceed directly to implementing the measure in accordance with the data and information provided if the affected state parties fail to respond within the notifying period of three months which can be extended by the Executive Secretariat.

225 Niger Basin Water Charter, art. 24; Lake Chad Basin Water Charter, art 60.

like the Niger Basin Water Charter, the notification period is three months and notification must be through the Senegal River Basin Commission (OMVS).[226]

The second trend on planned measures and exchange of information is that of the ambiguous and undefined process of notification under the Volta River Basin Convention and Volta Basin Code of Conduct. Both regimes recognize the need for notification of planned measures but fail to define the process of notification, period of notification, the parties to be notified, and the function of the RBO with respect to the notification.[227] This is similar to Article 9 of the UNECE Water Convention, which provides for different types of notification and the role of the joint bodies (or RBOs) without defining the process of notification.

3.4 *Emerging Principles*

Current shared watercourse regimes in Africa are proactive in recognizing principles for management of the transboundary watercourse beyond the universal principles set out in the UN Watercourses Convention and the UNECE Water Convention. While some of these principles are given limited recognition in the UN water treaties, most are peculiar to transboundary water resources management in the West Africa and are reflective of an original style,

226 Charter of Waters of the Senegal River, art. 24. Article 23 of the Niger Basin Water Charter provides that notification is through the Executive Secretariat of Niger Basin Authority while Article 54 of the Lake Chad Basin Water Charter provides for notification through the Lake Chad Basin Commission. The UN Watercourses Convention does not provide for notification through any established institution, but the role of joint bodies under Article 9 of the UNECE Water Convention is broad enough to encompass notification.

227 Article 4 of the Volta River Basin Convention provides that the principles of cooperation include general obligation to cooperate, regular exchange of data and information among states, consultation, negotiation and notification of planned activities that can have negative effects. However, the Convention fails to define the process of notification, the parties to be notified, and the approving authority. Although Article 6(1) and (3) mandates the Volta Basin Authority to promote permanent consultation tools among the parties and authorize the development of infrastructure and projects planned by stakeholders that could have a substantial impact on the water resources of the Basin, it is not clear who the stakeholders are. Article 21 of the Volta Basin Code of Conduct provides for notification on planned measures likely to harm the environment or water resources and further provides in Article 22 that the process of notification could lead to consultations and negotiations for equitable resolution. But the instrument does not provide for the means and process of notification; the role of its only organ, the Consultative Commission in the notification process is also not defined. The instrument fails to clarify whether notification should be to a particular state party and local population affected by the measure or to everybody in the river basin.

not as a result of influence of the UN water regimes These emerging principles of shared watercourse management are the human right to water, minimum streamflow, public participation, common works, and integrated basin management.

3.4.1 The Human Right to Water

Some of the shared watercourse regimes in West Africa recognize the concept of the human right to water similar to the provision found in the UN Watercourses Convention or even wider than it.[228] Article 15 of the Niger Basin Water Charter states the principle of 'no priority of use' of water except for 'essential human needs' which in the UN Watercourses Convention is known as 'vital human needs' and in the Volta Basin Code of Conduct as 'basic human needs.'[229] The Senegal River Water Charter gives preference to 'water for domestic uses,' which is broader than 'water for vital human needs.'[230] Water for vital human needs could be restricted to the most essential needs like drinking and cooking, which might not cover certain domestic uses of water. Article 1 of the South African Development Community (SADC) Water Protocol interprets 'domestic use of water' to mean "water for drinking, washing, cooking, bathing, sanitation and stock watering purposes."[231] Similarly, Section 2 of Nigeria Water Resources Act allows anyone to take water without charge for a 'domestic purpose' which by extension includes "water for watering livestock and for personal irrigation schemes." Article 8 of the Senegal River Water Charter also guarantees drinking water for the population, particularly, the most vulnerable and further includes water for agriculture as one of the most essential uses of the water resources. Similarly, the Lake Chad Basin Water Charter recognizes the concept of the human right to water very broadly. Accordingly, Article 72

228 The Charter of Waters of the Senegal River gives broader recognition to the human right to water than the UN Watercourses Convention.

229 Article 15 of the Niger Basin Water Charter and Article 25 of the Volta Basin Code of Conduct are similar to Article 10 of UN Watercourses Convention. As discussed above, this provision has been interpreted to mean water to meet essential human needs, including drinking water and water required for production of food in order to prevent death from dehydration and starvation.

230 Article 2 of the Charter of Waters of the Senegal River provides that distribution of water from the Senegal River shall be primarily for domestic uses. Article 10 provides that collection of water from the Basin is subject to prior authorization and possible fees except for water for domestic uses. With regard to the human right to water, the Senegal River Basin instrument is also consistent with the 2002 General Comment No. 15 on the Right to Water (n 163) which prefers the expression "water for personal and domestic uses."

231 SADC Water Protocol (n 164), art. 1.

of the Charter provides that "State Parties acknowledge that their people have a right to water and sanitation, which is a fundamental human right and is necessary for human dignity." Although the principle is merely acknowledged, the Lake Chad Basin instrument is the most recent of all the treaties and reflects the current position of the right to water as a human right.[232]

3.4.2 Minimum Streamflow

The need to sustain minimum streamflow of an international watercourse is codified in most shared watercourses regimes in West Africa under consideration. Streamflow protection is described as "a critical aspect of managing our waters in a sustainable manner."[233] According to the State of Vermont Watershed Management Division,

> in addition to minimum flows, the timing, frequency, duration and magnitude of both high and low flow events influence the physical and biological attributes of a stream or river. Changes in these characteristics can degrade habitat for fish and other aquatic organisms or affect their life cycles, result in increased erosion or sedimentation, and affect human use of rivers for recreation or other purposes.[234]

As rightly observed, the principle of minimum streamflow is compatible with the equitable and reasonable utilization principle because it is essential in protecting an international watercourse and necessary for resolving conflicts between human uses of the water and the water environment.[235] Further, the quantity of water in a watercourse is important to other casual users of water resources in the aquatic environment and for maintaining the integrity of the river channel.[236]

---

232 Article 2 of the Lake Chad Basin Water Charter defines 'right to water' as "supplies of physically accessible clean water of acceptable quality at an affordable cost, in sufficient amount to meet every person's personal and domestic needs." In 2010, through Resolution 64/292, the United Nations General Assembly recognized the human right to water and sanitation and acknowledged that clean drinking water and sanitation are part of the right to an adequate standard of living and are essential to the realization of all human rights.

233 'Streamflow Protection,' *State of Vermont, Agency of Natural Resources, Department of Environmental Conservation, Watershed Management Division*, http://dec.vermont.gov/watershed/rivers/streamflow-protection (accessed 11 September 2017).

234 Ibid.

235 Wouters & Vinogradov (n 131).

236 Ibid.

Both the Lake Chad Basin Water Charter and the Niger Basin Water Charter recognize the principle of minimum streamflow, though the former has more detailed provisions. Article 12 of the Lake Chad Basin Water Charter provides for "minimum flows to be maintained" during 'low waters' and 'high waters' while Appendix 2 of the Charter defines modalities for implementation of minimum streamflow including abstraction control.[237] Article 10 of Niger Basin Water Charter provides that "State Parties ... shall take all measures to preserve essential minimum stream flows" of Niger Basin water without any definition of such measures. Article 31 of the Volta Basin Code of Conduct creates the need for sustaining the 'environmental flow' of Volta River, which is similar to Article 10 of the Niger Basin Water Charter and more direct than the provision of the Senegal River Water Charter. Article 5(2) of the Senegal River Water Charter provides that integrated management of the water resource should consider the "availability and continuity of the resources" which is a soft recognition of minimum streamflow. The principle of minimum stream flow is recognized in some water regimes outside West Africa, but despite all the laudable provisions of both the UN Watercourses Convention and the UNECE Water Convention, neither treaty recognizes this very important principle.[238] Although the principle of protection of ecosystems under Article 20 of the UN Watercourses Convention seems to indirectly recognize preservation of minimum streamflow, this is not direct recognition.

3.4.3 Public Participation

The principle of public participation is another important feature of modern West African shared watercourse regimes. Since Agenda 21 and Principle 10 of the Rio Declarations[239] followed by the Aarhus Convention on Access to

237 Section 2 of the Lake Chad Water Charter has detailed provisions on 'abstraction management' in order to sustain the minimum streamflow while Article 41 makes specific provisions for prevention and management of low water levels and drought, all of which are mandatory provisions.

238 Article 6 of the Agreement on the Cooperation for the Sustainable Development of the Mekong River (Mekong River Basin Agreement) directly recognizes the need to maintain minimum stream flow of the Mekong River. The Mekong River Basin Agreement was adopted 5 April 1995, http://www.mrcmekong.org/assets/Publications/policies/agreement-Apr95.pdf. (accessed 28 August 2017).

239 Agenda 21 (n 156) and the Rio Declaration (n 157) were adopted at theUnited Nations Conference on Environment and Development (also known as the Earth Summit) held in Rio de Janeiro, Brazil (3 to 14 June 1992). Agenda 21 is a non-binding action plan on sustainable development. Relevant chapters on public participation regarding environmental matters are: Chapter 24 on Global Action for Women Towards Sustainable and

Information, Public Participation in Decision-Making and Access to Justice in Environmental Matters, were adopted, the principle of public participation has become relevant to environmental regimes, including transboundary watercourse governance.[240] The Aarhus Convention recognizes three levels of public participation: public access to information, public participation in decision-making, and public access to justice.[241] The rationale of the principle of public participation in the transboundary waters context is that the public who are the main users of the water resource should have the right to access the water, the right to information regarding the transboundary watercourse, and the right to participate in decision-making concerning the transboundary watercourse. This principle is consistent with the principle of the human right to water because it suggests that access to information and decision making regarding shared watercourses are not only for government officials of the basin states but also for the public. Accordingly, Tignino and Sangbana observe that projects on transboundary water resources can impact the living conditions and health of riparian populations, hence individuals and local communities increasingly have a role in environmental assessment of projects in the river basin.[242] Sangbana also observes that involving people at an early stage of the decision-making process in the shared watercourse creates greater trust in

---

Equitable Development; Chapter 25 on Children and Youth in Sustainable Development; Chapter 26 on Recognizing and Strengthening the Role of Indigenous People and Their Communities; Chapter 27 on Strengthening the Role of Non-Governmental Organizations: Partners for Sustainable Development; and Chapter 29 on Strengthening the Role of Workers and their Trade Unions. Principle 10 of the Rio Declaration states that "environmental issues are best handled with participation of all concerned citizens, at the relevant level. At the national level, each individual shall have appropriate access to information concerning the environment that is held by public authorities, including information on hazardous materials and activities in their communities, and the opportunity to participate in decision-making processes. States shall facilitate and encourage public awareness and participation by making information widely available. Effective access to judicial and administrative proceedings, including redress and remedy, shall be provided."

240 The Aarhus Convention was adopted 25 June 1998 and came into force 30 October 2001 (n 168).

241 Aarhus Convention (n 168) art. 1. Article 3 of the Convention on Environmental Impact Assessment in a Transboundary Context (Espoo Convention) is also relevant. Adopted on 25 February 1991 http://www.unece.org/env/eia/about/eia_text.html (accessed 15 January 2017).

242 M. Tignino & K. Sangbana, "L'eau, Les Individus et les Communautés Locales", *in* M. Tignino & K. Sangbana (eds), *Public Participation and Water Resources Management: Where Do We Stand in International Law?* pp. 12–16 (Paris, UNESCO, 2015) at 13.

the process, decreases the possibility of later conflicts, and guarantees preservation of their basic rights.[243]

Modern shared watercourse regimes in West Africa expressly recognize the right of the public to use water resources of the basin but, in addition recognize their rights to access information, participate in decision-making, and access justice. The only exception is the Volta River Basin Convention.[244] Perhaps the earliest and best recognition of the principle of public participation in the West African water regimes is the Senegal River Water Charter. As pointed out, the Senegal River regime statement on the human right to water is very generous. Furthermore, the preamble to the Charter acknowledges that sharing of the water resources should involve "users, managers, decision makers, developers and experts concerned." Article 2 of the Charter notes that one of its objectives is "to define the framework and participation of the water users in decision-making for the management of water resources of River Senegal." While Article 23 of the Charter provides the mode of public participation, Article 13 obliges coastal states to make accessible to the public information relating to the state of the water of the Senegal River to ensure regularity of flow of the Senegal River and information on the quality of the water.[245] Sangbana notes that granting observer status to members of the public by the Senegal River Basin regime also gives them direct access to the OMVS.[246]

The Niger Basin Water Charter codifies most elements of public participation reflected in the Senegal River Water Charter, and according to Dessouassi, integrated water resources management in the Niger River Basin is driven by participation of all stakeholders.[247] A major difference between these two instruments is that the Niger Basin regime also involves the public in settlement

---

243 Komlan Sangbana 'International Land Investments or the Environment Put up for Auction: The Case of the Niger Basin,' *in* F. Romanin Jacur et al. (eds), *Natural Resources Grabbing: An International Law Perspective*, pp. 181–98 (Leiden, Brill Nijhoff, 2016) at 193.

244 Article 6(3) of the Volta River Basin Convention recognizes participation of stakeholders in water management but fails to define 'the stakeholders' as members of the public.

245 Komlan Sangbana, "La Participation du Public dans le Cadre de l'Organisation pour la Mise en Valeur du Fleuve Sénégal" *in* Tinino & Sangbana (n 242) pp. 77–83 at 77 Article 23 of the Senegal River Water Charter provides that statute of observer may be granted to representatives of users, community representatives, Representatives of non-governmental organizations, and the Decentralized Management Committees.

246 Sangbana, ibid. at 79.

247 Robert Dessouassi, "État du Processus de Gestion Intégrée des Ressources en eau dans le Bassin du Niger: Expériences de l'Implication des Acteurs non Étatiques et de la Prévention des Conflits entre Usagers de Ressources", in Tinino & Sangbana (n 242), pp. 69–76 at 76.

of disputes.[248] Chapter VII (Articles 25 and 26) of the Niger Basin Water Charter guarantees public participation through access to information and further defines the extent of the participation.[249] Accordingly, the public has right "to be informed on the quality of water resources, to participate in both development and implementation of decisions relating to the basin and to access information on the condition of the transboundary waters, allocation of water to different sectors and the measures adopted to prevent, control and reduce transboundary impacts."[250] Further, "the right of public to access to information covers both all information on activities being implemented and planned measures which have a negative impact on the environment or human health in the basin," but this right is qualified by the exceptions listed in Article 203(7) of the Appendix.[251] The Lake Chad Basin Water Charter provision on public participation is different from that of both the Senegal and Niger River Basin regimes. Although, Chapter 12 of the Lake Chad Basin Water Charter defines the right of the basin population to include the right to water and sanitation as well as the right to public information and participation,[252] the right to public participation is made subject to the power of the Lake Chad Basin Commission to "establish a 'Public Participation Plan' which will determine the level and extent of public information and participation on water resources management." The implication is that until the LCBC completes the public participation plan, the public cannot exercise any right of participation.

---

248 Article 216 of the Protocol on Environment (Annex 1 of the Niger Basin Water Charter) permits customary and traditional authorities to participate in management and resolution of environmental conflicts at the local level.

249 The terms of public participation provided under Article 26 of the Niger Basin Water Charter are that information must be efficiently communicated from the beginning of the decision-making process; there should be reasonable time frames for the various stages of public participation; participation must start at the beginning of the procedure; the public needs to be informed promptly of new projects; the public must have the opportunity to submit in writing any observations, information, suggestions, proposals, counter-proposals, analyses or opinions that it considers relevant; states parties and the Authority should ensure that due account is taken of the results of public participation at the time of decision-making; and states parties shall ensure that, once a decision has been taken, the public shall be promptly informed.

250 Niger Basin Water Charter, art. 25.

251 Niger Basin Water Charter, art. 203(3) of the Appendix. Article 203(7) provides exceptions which include when the public authority does not hold the information, when application for the information is unreasonable, and when in the interest of a national law and public policy the information should be withheld.

252 Lake Chad Basin Water Charter, arts. 72 and 73.

The Volta Basin Code of Conduct expressly recognizes the principle of public participation in its provision that the states shall share the benefits of management of the water resources of the Volta River Basin with the local population.[253] It also recognizes the presence and good understanding of the local situation by local communities and therefore "involves stakeholders such as civil society groups, private sector, NGOs, community based organizations, traditional and customary authorities, women and youth groups to play key role in the management of water resources of the Basin."[254] However, the statement of recognition of the principle of public participation in the Volta River Basin Convention is brief and ambiguous. The Convention permits the Volta Basin Authority to authorize development of infrastructure and projects planned by stakeholders without defining who constitutes the stakeholders which could be members of the public or not.[255] Both the UN Watercourses Convention and UNECE Water Convention reflect limited recognition of the principle of public participation. The UN Watercourses Convention recognizes the principle only in the context of the human right to water and access of the public to claims or compensation due to any adverse activity in the watercourse within their territory.[256] The UNECE Water Convention grants access to information but without the right to participate in decision-making.[257]

3.4.4 Common Works

The principle of common works or structures is a unique feature of current shared watercourse regimes in West Africa, but as an emerging principle it is still developing and the extent of recognition across the different regimes varies. The first regime incorporating common works is the Convention Concerning the Legal Status of Common Works contracted by the Senegal River Basin states.[258] This was followed by the Gambia River Basin Convention on Common Structures. The Senegal River Basin regime on joint works defines some projects in the river basin as shared or joint works that are to be managed and financed jointly.[259] Apart from the Senegal River Basin and Gambia River Basin' regimes on common works, no other basin in West Africa has developed a separate instrument on joint works, but the principle is given adequate

253 Volta Basin Code of Conduct, art. 14.

254 Ibid., art. 15.

255 Ibid., art. 6(3).

256 UN Watercourses Convention, art. 10(2) and 32.

257 UNECE Water Convention, art. 16.

258 The Convention was adopted 21 December 1978.

259 For examples of common works see discussion on Article 3 of the Convention at note 63.

recognition within the water treaties. Further, only the Senegal River Basin regime confers the status of joint work to any project in the Basin. According to Tignino, "Niger River basin states are still at the beginning of a shared vision process for jointly managed infrastructure and equitable benefit sharing, while Senegal River basin states have led the way in innovative forms of shared ownership and governance."[260]

Article 1 of the Niger Basin Water Charter specifies two types of shared works: common facility or joint work owned by all party states and facilities of common interest or works of interest to two or more states but managed by the Niger Basin Authority.[261] The importance of common works is further reflected in the principle of shared vision or benefit sharing, and Article 27 of the Charter allows implementation of shared works projects in the Basin. While there is currently no common facility or joint works in the Niger River Basin, some works, (Fomi, Taossa and Kandadji Dams) are designated works of common interest "within the framework of the Basin Sustainable Development Action Plan."[262] The provisions of the Niger Basin Water Charter are slightly better than those of the Lake Chad Basin regime. The latter's provision that "State Parties may decide to construct common facilities or facilities of common interest for the sustainable management of the Basin"[263] is very uncertain and futuristic. The principle of joint works is also recognized in the Volta River Basin Convention, but it is briefly stated as one of the mandates of the Volta Basin Authority.[264] It is not reflected in any way in the Volta Basin Code of Conduct and is not listed as one of the joint actions of the parties under Part IV of the instrument. To date, the Senegal River Basin regime on joint works best recognizes the principle in West Africa.

3.4.5 Integrated Basin Management

A key driver of sustainable development in the shared watercourses in West Africa is the principle of integrated basin management, which is reflected in the current shared watercourse regimes. Integrated basin management means

260 Mara Tignino, 'Joint Infrastructure and the Sharing of Benefits in the Senegal and Niger Watersheds,' *Water International*, Vol. 41, No. 6 (2016), pp. 835–50 at abstract.

261 Observed by Tignino and Sagbana (n 67).

262 Tignino and Sangbana (ibid.) at 3.

263 Unlike Article 67 of the Lake Chad Basin Water Charter, Article 27 of Niger Basin Water Charter provides that some facilities built in the River Basin "may obtain the status of common facilities or facilities of common interest."

264 Article 6 of the Volta River Basin Convention defines the mandate of the Volta Basin Authority to include "to develop joint projects and works."

management of the basin with consideration of other factors that affect the river basin and its ecosystems.[265] This is also a major tenet of the Convention on Biological Diversity.[266] According to Sangbana, RBOs play a central role in integrated management of the different basins.[267] Accordingly, Article 6 of the Volta River Basin Convention states that one of the mandates of the Volta Basin Authority is "to promote the implementation of integrated water resources management and the equitable distribution of the benefits resulting from their various utilization." Like the Volta River Basin Convention, other regimes like the Niger Basin Water Charter recognize the importance of integrated basin management without stating the necessary factors.[268] The only exception is the Senegal River Water Charter which is considered to best recognize integrated basin management in the region. According to Ayibotele, the water resources of the Senegal River Basin are jointly managed to meet the socio-economic development needs of the riparian states and to ensure the integrity of the environment.[269] Article 5 of the Charter sets out the need to integrate various elements in distribution of water resources and also provides the factors for integrated management of the water resources in the River Basin.[270] These factors resemble the criteria for equitable and reasonable

265 According to the WWF "Integrated river basin management (IRBM) is the process of coordinating conservation, management and development of water, land and related resources across sectors within a given river basin, in order to maximise the economic and social benefits derived from water resources in an equitable manner while preserving and, where necessary, restoring freshwater ecosystems." 'Integrated River Basin Management (IRBM): A Holistic Appoach,' *WWF*, http://wwf.panda.org/about_our_earth/about_freshwater/rivers/irbm/ (accessed 25 January 2017).

266 The Convention on Biological Diversity was adopted at Rio de Janeiro, 5 June 1992. https://www.cbd.int/doc/legal/cbd-en.pdf (accessed 25 January 2017).

267 Sangbana, (n 35).

268 The preamble to the Niger Basin Water Charter states that the goal of the 'shared vision' principle is to make "the Niger Basin a common area of sustainable development by the integrated management of the water resources and associated ecosystems for the improvement of living conditions and prosperity of the populations."

269 Ayibotele (n 34).

270 Under Article 5(2) of the Charter of Waters of the Senegal River, the integrated management of the resource will take into account: the availability and the continuity of the resource; the integration of the dimension of the environment in the management of water and the durable maintenance of the favorable ecological conditions in the basin of the River; the irrigation of a maximum quantity of surfaces according to the availability of the resource; permanent navigability of the river; optimal exploitation of the hydroelectric potential energy available; the creation of the hydraulic conditions necessary to the flood of the Valley and the traditional cultures of fall; the rolling of the exceptional

utilization of water resources set out in Article 6 of the UN Watercourses Convention. Similarly, the UNECE Water Convention is a basin management instrument that linked to the principle of integrated water resources management (IWRM), which covers both the watercourse and land activities.[271]

3.5 *Institutional Aspects under West African Transboundary Water Treaties*

Like the UNECE Water Convention, all of the current West African water treaties recognize the need for a river basin organization or joint water commission, but their composition differs.[272] The Convention also recognized that joint commissions "may vary according to specific needs of the riparian States involved, but the majority of them share common features."[273] Consistent with

---

natural risings with Manantali, and the reduction of the risks of flood; improvement of the filling of the Lakes Guiers and the R' Kiz, as well as natural depressions; and reasonable requests by the economic sector and their implications.

271 Article 2 (6) of UNECE Water Convention encourages riparian states to develop policies and programs that cover 'relevant catchment areas'.

272 The UN Watercourses Convention has no mandatory provisions for the institutional framework for management of an international watercourse. Article 8(2) and 24 (1) suggest that parties could establish a 'joint management mechanism'. In West African water regimes, the composition of the institutional organs are not similar. Article 3 of Volta River Basin Convention includes the 'Forum of Parties' as an organ of Volta Basin Authority which is not a feature of any other institution in the region. Article 7 of the Convention for the Establishment of the Organization for the Development of the Senegal River (OMVS) has a Standing Committee on the Waters while Article IV of the Koliba-Korubal River Protocol includes representatives of donor agencies on the Permanent Technical Committee. The basin institutions are established within most of the water treaties but the Senegal and Gambia River Basins have separate instruments for the institutional framework which are Convention Relating to the Creation of the Gambia River Basin Development Organisation and Convention for the Establishment of the Organization for the Development of the Senegal River.

273 According to the UNECE (n 117 at 71), the common features of a joint water commission are: a permanent body meeting at reasonably regular intervals; composed of representatives of the riparian states, headed usually by officials, authorized for that purpose by governments; country representation in a joint commission is not necessarily limited to representatives of water authorities and may also include officials from various ministries and agencies, regional and local or municipal authorities; may have a decision-making body/ies, an executive body(ies) and subsidiary bodies, e.g. working or expert groups, monitoring, data collection and processing units; and a secretariat. The work of the joint commissions may be supplemented by the establishment of an auditing commission, a network of national offices, a consultative group of donors, an information centre, a training centre or observers. Recent practice shows that joint commissions increasingly allow

this observation, the West Africa joint water institutions or RBOs share common features but differ in composition.

The first major trend is that of treaties with defined institution comprising of several organs. The Niger Basin Water Charter, Volta River Basin Convention, the Lake Chad Basin Water Charter and the Senegal River Water Charter fall into this category. The main institution for the management of water resources of Niger River Basin is the Niger Basin Authority (NBA).[274] The NBA comprises four organs: the Summit of Heads of State and Government; the Council of Ministers; the Technical Committee of Experts; and the Executive Secretariat. Similarly, Article 82 of the Lake Chad Basin Water Charter creates main and subsidiary organs for implementing the Charter but these are not expressly stated as organs of the Lake Chad Basin Commission (LCBC). Article 8 of the Fort Lamy Convention established the LCBC which comprises eight members (two persons per member state).[275] Although, the provision concerning institutional organs of the Lake Chad Basin Water Charter is more detailed than that of the Niger Basin Water Charter, the former fails to define the relationship between the organs established for implementing the Charter and the already existing institution of the LCBC. Article 5 of the Convention Creating the Niger Basin Authority clearly defines the institutions as organs of the NBA. The Niger Basin Water Charter improved on this provision through its creation of the Permanent Technical Committee. The role of the Committee is to implement the Water Charter, to act as advisory body to the Executive Secretariat, and to assume responsibility, among others, for equitable water use.[276] It also plays a key role in dispute resolution.[277] However the Charter fails to define the composition of the Committee.

for the participation of representatives from the private sector and the public, including NGOS.

274 Article 1 of the Convention Creating the Niger Basin Authority establishes the Niger Basin Authority and Article 5 defines its composition.

275 Article 82 of the Lake Chad Basin Water Charter sets out the main organs for its implementation: the Summit of Heads of State, the Council of Ministers and Executive Secretariat as well as its subsidiary organs: the Technical Committee, Regional Parliamentary Committee, Water Resources Advisory Committee, Environment, Science and Planning Advisory Committee, National Agencies of the Lake Chad Basin Commission (National LCBC Agencies) and the Lake Chad Basin Forum of Sustainable Development Partners.

276 Niger Basin Water Charter, arts. 16 and 17.

277 Article 30 of the Niger Basin Water Charter provides that where parties cannot resolve their dispute amicably, it should be submitted to the Permanent Technical Committee, which will propose a settlement to the Council of Ministers.

The Volta River Basin Convention follows the trend of the Niger Basin Water Charter and includes the 'Forum of Parties' as one of its organs.[278] This is like the 'Meeting of Parties' in Article 17 of the UNECE Water Convention. This is different from the provision of the Senegal River Water Charter which retained the 'Permanent Organs' established under Article 7 of the Convention Pertaining to the Creation of the Organization for the Management of the Senegal River (OMVS). They are the Council of Ministers, the Office and the Standing Committee of the Waters. Unlike the Gambia River Basin treaty, which has a similar provision, the supreme body of the OMVS, the Conference of Heads of State and Government, is not part of its permanent organs.[279] The Standing Committee of Waters is an unique provision of the Senegal River Water regime and it is composed of representatives of riparian states.[280] Article 19 of the Senegal River Water Charter defines the role of the Standing Committee of Water which is similar to the role of the Permanent Technical Committee under Article 17 of the Niger Basin Water Charter and joint bodies recognized by the UNECE Water Convention.[281] The Standing Committee of Water also functions as advisory body to the Council of Ministers on works and projects in the Senegal River Basin.[282] The Senegal River regime involves the public in its institutional framework through the status of observer which work with the Standing Committee of Water.[283]

---

278 Article 3 of the Convention on the Status of the Volta River creates the Volta Basin Authority (VBA) and its organs: the Assembly of Heads of State, Council of Ministers in charge of Water Resources, Forum of the Parties, Committee of Experts, and the Executive Directorate of the Authority.

279 Under Articles 6 and 7 of the Convention Pertaining to the Creation of the Organization for the Management of the Senegal River (OMVS), the permanent organs of the OVMS are the Council of Ministers, the Office and the Standing Committee of the Waters. Article 3 of the Convention Relating to the Creation of the Gambia Basin Development Organisation established the Gambia Basin Development Organisation (OMVG) with its permanent organs as the Conference of Heads of States and Government, Council of Ministers, the High Commission and Permanent Water Commission.

280 Charter of Waters of the Senegal River, art. 20.

281 The Standing Committee of Water is responsible for the distribution of water between the various sectors of use. Similarly, in Article 17 of the Niger Basin Water Charter, the Permanent Technical Committee is responsible for ensuring the rational and equitable use of water of the Niger Basin under the rules agreed upon by member states. Article 9 of the UNECE Water Convention provides that the 'joint bodies' are responsibility for "joint monitoring programmes concerning water quality and water quantity."

282 Charter of Waters of the Senegal River, art. 21.

283 Article 23 provides that status of observer can be granted to representatives of the users; local authorities; non-governmental organizations and the Board of Decentralised Management (See footnote 245).

The second trend in the institutional framework of the current water regimes in West Africa is demonstrated by the Volta Basin Code of Conduct, which lacks defined structures, and composition of its only institution, the Consultative Commission, which is only responsible for implementing the instrument.[284] With the detailed provisions of the Volta River Basin Convention regarding an institutional framework, the scanty provisions of the Code of Conduct which is soft law and not inclusive of all riparian states is not very material to this analysis.

3.6 *Dispute Settlement Mechanisms within West African Transboundary Water Treaties*

Dispute settlement is one of the earliest features of instruments for transboundary water management in West Africa[285] and is consistently recognized in current regimes as modified.[286] The current dispute resolution provisions are divided between instruments with detailed procedures for dispute resolution (as provided in Article 33 of the UN Watercourses Convention), such as the Niger Basin Water Charter, Lake Chad Basin Water Charter, and Volta River Basin Convention, and instruments with brief dispute resolution provisions (similar to Article 22 of the UNECE Water Convention), such as the Senegal River water Charter, and the Volta Basin Code of Conduct.

Although the Niger Basin Water Charter and Lake Chad Basin Water Charter follow the process of dispute settlement set out in Article 33 of the UN Watercourses Convention, Article 29 of the Niger Basin Water Charter encourage parties to utilize the good offices of the Niger Basin Authority, mediation, conciliation, or 'any other peaceful means' to resolve their differences. What is meant by 'any other peaceful' is uncertain; it could be negotiation or another means of dispute resolution, and it could be interpreted to be with or without the supervision of the NBA. Further provisions of the Charter allow the NBA to submit the dispute to the Permanent Technical Committee who will recommend resolution by the Council of Ministers or Summit of Heads of State and Government. The recommendation must be concluded within six months of submission.[287] If the parties can still not resolve the dispute, they shall refer it to the Conciliation Commission of the African Union before proceeding to the International Court of Justice. The provision of the Lake Chad

284 Volta River Basin Code of Conduct, arts. 51 and 52.

285 Bamako Convention, art. 17; Act of Niamey, art. 7.

286 Most early post-colonial treaties recognize one or two levels of dispute resolution. Article 17 of the Bamako Convention provides for amicable dispute settlement and arbitration.

287 Niger Basin Water Charter, art. 30.

Basin Water Charter is a bit different. Article 86 of the Charter allows parties to start the dispute resolution by direct negotiation before approaching the Lake Chad Basin Commission, which shall utilize its good offices or mediation for settlement of the dispute. Thereafter any party can bring the dispute to the "competent regional and sub-regional authorities."[288] Unlike the Niger Basin Water Charter, the Lake Chad Basin Water Charter fails to name the competent authorities leaving an ambiguous gap.[289] At this point, the parties could decide to submit the dispute to the International Court of Justice for arbitration or judicial resolution. The process of dispute resolution in the Volta River Basin Treaty is clearer. The process must start with mediation and conciliation within the Volta Basin Authority (VBA). In other treaties, the parties are permitted to arrange for mediation or conciliation before proceeding to the institutional body. If the VBA cannot resolve the dispute amicably, parties can submit the dispute to one of the competent organs of ECOWAS or the African Union and thereafter to the International Court of Justice.[290]

The second trend in dispute resolution in the regimes is shown by the brief and ambiguous provisions of the Senegal River Water Charter and the Volta Basin Code of Conduct. In the Senegal River regime, the process starts with conciliation and mediation and can proceed to the Commission of Conciliation and Arbitration of the African Union and then to the International Court of Justice.[291] The river basin organization (OMVS) is not included in the process of dispute resolution, and it is not clear how the parties will initiate the conciliation or mediation process. Article 55 of the Volta Basin Code of Conduct provides that states should refer dispute to the Consultative Commission and thereafter recommends resolution by the use of diplomatic channels through the Ministers of Foreign Affairs. The expression 'diplomatic channel' is vague, and the instrument does not provide for any other stage of dispute resolution.

3.7 *West African Water Regimes Versus the UN Water Treaties*

Globally, there is no perfect water regime. Although international water law provides the essential principles of a good transboundary water instrument,

288 Lake Chad Basin Water Charter, art. 88.

289 Some relevant 'competent regional and sub-regional authorities' are the Economic Community on West African States (ECOWAS), African Union (AU) and the African Ministers' Council on Water (AMCOW).

290 Convention on the Status of the Volta River, art. 13.

291 Charter of Waters of the Senegal River, art. 30: Convention Relating to Status of River Gambia, art. 18.

most treaties, including the UN water treaties, have loopholes.[292] Both the old and current West African water instruments have been criticized, and there is need for improvement in the region.[293] It has been suggested that a global convention like the UN Watercourses Convention

> will serve in West Africa as a binding denominator among co-riparian States containing minimum cooperation standards; progressively spur the revision and strengthening of existing watercourse agreements and the adoption of new basin-specific treaties where none exists; and improve dialogue and cooperation between ECOWAS member States and non-members sharing water resources within the region.[294]

Current shared watercourse regimes in West Africa have improved on earlier instruments; primarily due to the influence of the UN water treaties, particularly the UN Watercourses Convention. However, there are still areas where there is a need for additional changes, particularly to regimes with major failings and in basins without instruments. There is also a need to include riparian states who are not party to current regimes and to harmonize multiple regimes for major river basins in the West Africa.[295] Experience in the region

292 The UNECE Water Convention has been criticized for its limited codification of substantive norms while the UN Watercourses Convention lacks detailed provisions on institutional frameworks.

293 Garane (n 27) at 28–30.

294 ECOWAS et al. (n 24) at 4.

295 Algeria, a riparian state of the Niger River Basin is not party to the Niger Basin Water Charter; Guinea and Guinea Bissau are not parties to the Charter of Waters of the Senegal River although they are parties to earlier instruments like the Bamako Convention adopted in 1963, the Convention Relating to the Status of the Senegal River adopted in 1964 and the General Scheme for Development of the Senegal River Basin adopted in 1970. The regime of the Niger River Basin includes the Niger Basin Water Charter adopted on 30 April 2008; Revised Convention Pertaining to Creating the Niger Basin Authority adopted in 1987; Convention Creating the Niger Basin Authority adopted in 1980; and Protocol of the Agreement between the Republic of Niger and the Republic of Mali Relative to Cooperation in the Utilization of Water Resources of the Niger River, adopted on 7 December 1988 (http://ocid.nacse.org/tfdd/tfdddocs/468FRE.pdf); Agreement between the Federal Republic of Nigeria and the Republic of Niger concerning the Equitable Sharing in the Development, Conservation and use of their Common Water Resources adopted on 18 August 1990 (http://ocid.nacse.org/tfdd/tfdddocs/483ENG.pdf); Agreement between the Republic of Niger and the Republic of Benin relative to the Realization of the Hydroelectric Management of the Dyondyonga Site on the Mékrou river, adopted on 14 January 1999 (http://ocid.nacse.org/tfdd/treaties.php?page=full&origin=river&tn=600);

has shown that the greater the influence of the UN water treaties, the better the water regime.[296] However the potential benefit of the two UN water treaties in the region varies and their application depends on several factors including relevance and acceptability. It is important to determine whether the two treaties are valuable to the West Africa region and to what extent.

Regarding the scope of application of transboundary water instruments, both the UN Watercourses Convention and the UNECE Water Convention are capable of improving the scope of the West Africa water treaty regimes. However, the UNECE Water Convention is more beneficial because of its wider scope, which includes confined and unconfined groundwater. The Lake Chad Basin Water Charter is the only regime that covers both surface water and all groundwater. Substantive provisions are better enunciated in the UN Watercourses Convention than the UNECE Water Convention so the UN Watercourses Convention could correct the defects in the substantive provisions of most water treaties in West Africa and also serve as a model to provide guidance to basins without treaties. Regarding procedural obligations, instruments influenced by the provisions of the UN water treaties have better codification of procedural principles. Articles 12 to 19 of the UN Watercourses Convention present a defined process of notification of planned measures that are reflected in some treaties like the Niger Basin Water Charter and the Lake Chad Basin Water Charter. The UNECE Water Convention recognizes the need for notification but does not present any process of notification. Its main benefit to West Africa is the definition of the functions of the joint bodies or the RBOs regarding notification.[297] Both treaties will improve the procedural rules of the water treaty regimes of West Africa, but the UN Watercourses Convention, which clearly sets out the principle of obligation to cooperate and the process of planned measures notification, is preferable. Some elements of cooperation and notification within Article 9 of the UNECE Water Convention might be too 'foreign' or complex for West Africa.[298]

---

and the Memorandum of Understanding between the Republic of Niger and the Republic of Mali on the Construction of Dams Taoussa in Mali and Kandadji in Niger signed on 6 June 2004. (http://ocid.nacse.org/tfdd/treaties.php?page=full&origin=river&tn=630).

296 Examples are the Lake Chad Basin Water Charter and the Niger Basin Water Charter.

297 Aricle 9(2)(h) of the UNECE Water Convention provides that the joint bodies will "serve as a forum for the exchange of information on existing and planned uses of water and related installations that are likely to cause transboundary impact."

298 Article 9 of the UNECE Water Convention sets out the role of the joint bodies: to develop concerted action programs for the reduction of pollution loads from both point sources (e.g. municipal and industrial sources) and diffuse sources (particularly from agriculture),

Article 33 of the UN Watercourses Convention provides different types and procedures of dispute resolution not recognized by the UNECE Water Convention. The UNECE Water Convention provides very limited forms of dispute resolution and so will not offer any additional benefits to the West African water treaty regime. Regarding the institutional framework, Article 24 of the UN Watercourses Convention encourages riparian states to have a 'joint management mechanism,' but Article 9 of the UNECE Water Convention makes it mandatory. Most of the West African water treaties considered in this study have institutional bodies for management of the transboundary watercourse, but other river basins in the region are without instruments and basin organizations. It is good to have a RBO, but according to Garane, the mandatory requirement of a RBO under the UNECE Water Convention is unrealistic because many riparian states in West Africa do not have resources to sustain such an organization.[299] Nonetheless, it is worse to leave the basins unregulated, hence the UN water treaties offer the opportunity to apply the universal principles set out above. In a basin,

> where an agreement is in place, universal principles and rules can help to clarify its content. Where no agreement is in place, these principles and rules provide guidance on how sustainable management on shared freshwater systems should be carried out.[300]

The slow ratification process of the UN Watercourses Convention demonstrates that states are reluctant "to conclude instruments on transboundary freshwater resources at the universal level," but are more willing to translate the universal norms in the global instruments to specific norms at the regional or basin level.[301] According to Boisson de Chazournes, "universal instruments and norms have helped to shape the content of instruments adopted at the regional and basin level."[302] Consistent with this position, most basin-specific regimes in West Africa were improved with the application of the universal

---

promote the cooperation and exchange of information on the best available technology in accordance with the provisions of Article 13 of the Convention, and to encourage cooperation in scientific research programmes. These programs appear to be too 'European' for West Africa.

299 Garane (n 27).

300 Boisson de Chazournes (n 3) at 10.

301 Ibid. at 2.

302 Ibid. at 5.

provisions of the UN Watercourses Convention.[303] Furthermore, some water regimes at the basin level have codified the important principles of common works, minimum streamflow and public participation, principles that are not fully developed in either UN water treaty. Boisson de Chazournes also observed that "agreements adopted at the basin level reflect the specific characteristics of the watercourse they apply to"[304] but as earlier noted most West African states cannot afford the cost of regulating every shared watercourse. Nevertheless, to address the problems of non-regulation of basins in West Africa, the need to include all riparian states in the basin regime, and harmonization of multiple shared watercourse instruments in the region, a regional treaty like the UNECE Water Convention and the Revised Protocol on Shared Watercourses in the Southern African Development Community (SADC Protocol) is recommended. Although the influence of the UN Watercourses Convention in the region is established, the influence of the UNECE Water Convention is very minimal, and its potential benefits are yet to be determined.

4.0 Assessment of the UNECE Water Convention Framework of Implementation from the West African Perspective

The UN Watercourses Convention and the UNECE Water Convention are different instruments though their provisions are not conflicting. While the former is global in scope from the onset, the latter started as a regional regime. Because of the differences between the two conventions, this section will consider if the UNECE Water Convention is a legitimate instrument for West Africa. According to Thomas Frank,

> the effectiveness or 'compliance-pull' of a rule will hinge on how legitimate the rule is perceived to be by the subjects it is meant to govern. Legitimacy, in Frank's view, is contingent on four independent factors, including the clarity of the rule, the consistency with which the rule is

303 The Senegal River Water Charter improved on the principle of the human right to water stated in Article 10 of the UN Watercourses Convention. Furthermore, both the Niger Basin Water Charter and the Lake Chad Basin Water Charter enunciate more principles for equitable and reasonable utilization than provided in Article 6 of the UN Watercourses Convention.

304 Boisson de Chazournes (n 3) at 5.

> applied and the degree to which a new rule fits with existing accepted practice or rules about how rules are made.[305]

It is necessary to consider how the UNECE Water Convention can add value to transboundary water management and cooperation in West Africa. Three issues will be considered here: identifying key activities (guidelines, recommendations and programs etc.) that have been conducted in support of implementing the UNECE Water Convention; assessing whether and to what extent similar activities are already taking place in West Africa through other bodies outside the UNECE; and where there are gaps, considering whether the projects and programs under the UNECE Water Convention would offer solutions to problems specific to West Africa.

4.1 *Institutional Framework under the UNECE Water Convention*

One major achievement of the UNECE Water Convention is its strong legal and institutional framework, in particular the Meeting of parties every three years which is the major institution for implementing the provisions of the Convention.[306] It is supported by other institutions, namely the Bureau, the Legal Board, Implementation Committee, task force,[307] working groups[308] and the Secretariat (Figure 3). Over the course of the last twenty years, "these institutional arrangements have proven highly effective in constantly assessing and strengthening the implementation of the UNECE Water Convention at the basin and national levels."[309] The UNECE Meeting of parties is a key

305 Thomas Frank as cited in Christiana Ochoa, 'Corporate Social Responsibility and Firm Compliance: Lessons from the International Law-International Relations Discourse,' *Santa Clara Journal of International Law*, Vol. 9 (2011), pp. 169–78 at 174.

306 According to Rieu-Clarke, the role of the UNECE Meeting of Parties is "for defining and reviewing the activities and policies under the Convention as well as sharing information on experience gained in negotiating, and implementing bilateral and multilateral agreements concerning transboundary waters." Alistair Rieu-Clarke 'Transboundary Water Sharing and Conflict: A Review of Best Practice' (Centre for Water Law, Policy and Science, University of Dundee, 2009) at 13.

307 Task Force on Water and Climate and Global Network of Basins, Task Force on Water-Food-Energy, and Joint Ad Hoc Expert Groups on Water and Industrial Accidents.

308 Working Group on Integrated Water Resources Management, Working Group on Monitoring and Assessment and the International Water Assessment Centre.

309 UN Watercourses Convention online Users' Guide, 'The Relationship with the UNECE Convention' http://www.unwatercoursesconvention.org/importance/the-relationship-with-the-unece-water-convention/ (accessed 22 September 2017).

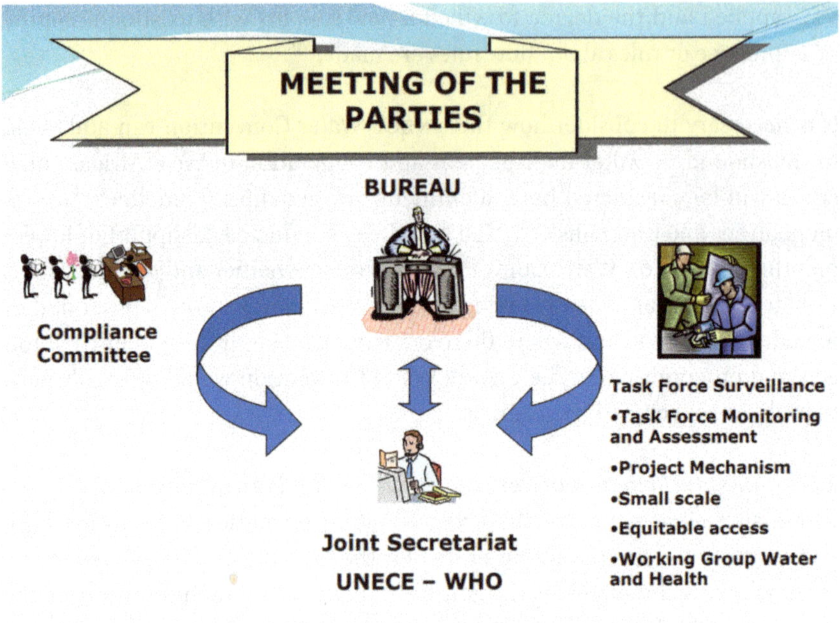

FIGURE 3 *Institutional structure under the* UNECE *Water Convention.*
SOURCE: UNECE (2014)

activity under the Convention with potential value to West African transboundary water management. Party states to the UNECE Water Convention have developed strong links with non-party states who are invited to the Meeting. Participation in such a gathering could strengthen relationships between states in West Africa and countries outside West Africa sharing the same water resources.[310]

Some institutions in West Africa that are similar to the UNECE Meeting of Parties are the ECOWAS, the African Ministers' Council on Water (AMCOW), and the institutional bodies of different river basins. Most West African states are members of the strong regional body, ECOWAS, whose main mission is to promote "economic integration in all fields of activity of the constituting countries" including water resources.[311] ECOWAS is composed of 15 out of the

310 Part of Cameroon and Algeria have coastline on the Niger Basin, though the countries are not considered to be in West Africa. The Central African Republic is on the Lake Chad Basin while Mauritania shares the Atui River with Western Sahara in North Africa.

311 ECOWAS, 'Basic Information,' http://www.ecowas.int/about-ecowas/basic-information (accessed 12 September 2017). The ECOWAS Water Resources Co-ordination Centre is located in Ouagadougou, Burkina Faso.

18 countries that make up West Africa. Like the UNECE, which undertakes activities to manage transboundary water resources between UNECE and non-UNECE states, ECOWAS could adopt a water treaty to serve as a platform for cooperation between its member states and states outside ECOWAS that share water resources. Major achievements of ECOWAS in the field of water resources development include the formulation of the ECOWAS Water Policy, establishment of the ECOWAS Co-ordination Centre which has piloted projects including a climate change project titled 'Water, Food and Energy Security,'[312] and establishment of the Regional Water Information Centre.

West African States are also members of AMCOW[313] whose primary purpose is "to promote cooperation, security, social and economic development and poverty eradication among member states through the effective management of the continent's water resources and provision of water supply services."[314] AMCOW influences water resources management and development through organizing and hosting African Water Week every two years, formulating water resources policies, and serving as a link to other similar bodies outside Africa.

With these two strong institutional bodies in West Africa and the river basin organizations discussed above, do states in West Africa need to become a party to the UNECE Water Convention? Although the Meeting of Parties is a good example of a strong regional institution, it is not clear that states in West Africa need to participate in it.

---

312 Other projects are the Establish a Hunger-free Initiative for Africa (piloted with FAO) and the Regional Water Observatory Project to facilitate joint action on transboundary water resources management. See 'ECOWAS: The Establishment of a Regional Water Observatory,' *African Water Facility* (1 August 2011), http://www.africanwaterfacility.org/en/projects/project/ecowas-the-establishment-of-a-regional-water-observatory-139/ (accessed 17 January 2017).

313 AMCOW comprises the Ministers responsible for water in forty-one African countries. It was launched at the Conference of Ministers of Water in Africa held in Abuja, Nigeria, 29–30 April 2002. The AMCOW Secretariat is in Abuja, Nigeria and is headed by an Executive Secretary and support staff. The AMCOW institutional set-up consists of the AMCOW Governing Council, the "principal inter-governmental body on water issues and is composed of all 53 African Ministers responsible for water affairs in the region"; the AMCOW Executive Committee which "comprises the President of the Council and 15 other members—three members elected from each of the five sub-regions of Africa on a rotational basis" (AMCOW member states are divided into five sub-regions: West Africa, Eastern Africa, Central Africa, North Africa and Southern Africa); and the AMCOW Technical Advisory Committee (TAC) which "comprises 25 technical experts, 5 from each of the five sub-regions of Africa, on a rotational basis." See African Ministers' Council on Water http://www.amcow-online.org/index.php?option=com_content&view=article&id=115&Itemid=71&lang=en (accessed 12 September 2017).

314 Ibid.

4.2 *Legal and Institutional Arrangements under Article 9 of the* UNECE *Water Convention*

Article 9 of the UNECE Water Convention mandates riparian states to manage transboundary watercourses through agreements and river basin joint bodies at the catchment or river basin level. According to Nikiforova, one of the major activities of the Convention is the establishment of agreements and joint bodies for different river basins.[315] A good framework agreement, the UNECE Water Convention has aided and served as a model for several bilateral and multilateral treaties in the UNECE region. Examples include the Convention on Co-operation for the Protection and Sustainable Use of the River Danube between 11 countries and European Union (EU),[316] the Convention on the Protection of the Rhine signed by the five riparian states and the EU[317] and the EU Water Framework Directive.[318] Parties to the UNECE Water Convention have also adopted two protocols: the Protocol on Water and Health, and the Protocol on Civil Liability and Compensation for Damage Caused by the Transboundary Effects of Industrial Activities on Transboundary Waters.[319] The UNECE Water Convention has been described as "a unique framework instrument that places much emphasis on and provides mechanisms for developing institutional cooperation between countries."[320] The benefits of

315 Nataliya Nikiforova, '20 years' Experience in Implementing the UNECE Water Convention.' Presentation at the 5th Annual International Water Law and Transboundary Freshwaters Workshop, Dundee, 9–13 June 2014.

316 Convention on Cooperation for the Protection and Sustainable Development of the River Danube, Sofia, 24 June 1994, http://faolex.fao.org/docs/pdf/mul17444.pdf. (accessed 26 February 2017). Party states are Austria, Bulgaria, Croatia, the Czech Republic, Germany, Hungary, Moldova, Romania, Slovakia, Slovenia and Ukraine.

317 Convention on the Protection of the Rhine, Rotterdam, 22 January 1998. http://www.internationalwaterlaw.org/documents/regionaldocs/rhine_river.html. (accessed 26 February 2017). Party states are Switzerland, France, Germany, Luxembourg, the Netherlands and the EU.

318 The European Union Directive 2000/60/EC of the European Parliament and of the Council of 23 October 2000 establishing a framework for Community action in the field of water policy. http://ec.europa.eu/environment/water/water-framework/index_en.html (accessed 17 September 2017).

319 Protocol on Water and Health, London, 17 June 1999, https://www.unece.org/fileadmin/DAM/env/documents/2000/wat/mp.wat.2000.1.e.pdf (accessed 26 February 2017); Protocol on Civil Liability, Kiev, 22 May 2003, not in force, http://www.unece.org/fileadmin/DAM/env/civil-liability/documents/protocol_e.pdf (accessed 26 February 2017).

320 UNECE. *River Basin Commissions and Other Institutions for Transboundary Water Cooperation*, (New York & Geneva, United Nations, 2009) at 8.

the Convention are in its mandatory provisions, which include joint institutions and the exchange of information.

As discussed above, although six major transboundary watersheds in West Africa have treaties, the provisions of most of these treaties do not cover all the principles of transboundary water management or only partially do so.[321] According to Garane, many of the agreements "do not address important aspects of international water law."[322] River basins like the Cross River Basin, the Akpi Yafi River Basin, and Mono River Basin do not have a treaty, while some with agreements, such as the Koliba-Korubal River Protocol and the Gambia River Basin Treaty, have major flaws. The ECOWAS Water Policy is not yet a binding treaty so it cannot address the lapses and lack of uniformity in water treaty regimes in West Africa. In spite of all the benefits of establishing a joint basin agreement and organization for every river basin in West Africa, the mandatory requirement under Article 9 of the UNECE Water Convention will be too burdensome for West Africa because most countries in the region lack the necessary financial and technical resources to establish such an organization.[323] This reality makes enforcement of this provision for every river basin premature and almost impossible in West Africa.

4.3 *Transboundary Groundwater Management under the UNECE Water Convention*

Another key activity under the UNECE Water Convention that could benefit West Africa relates to groundwater assessment activities, quantifying the benefits of transboundary water cooperation, and application of the provisions of the soft law, Model Provisions on Transboundary Groundwater. Under the implementation policies of the UNECE Water Convention, monitoring and assessment of both surface water and groundwater are the basis of management of a shared watercourse. The influence of the Convention for transboundary water cooperation extends to Central Asia through the UNECE-GIZ project titled, 'Regional Dialogue and Cooperation on Water Resources Management,' which focuses on four programs in the Aral Sea Basin (2011–2015): integrated water resources management, environmental protection, socio-economic

321 The Charter of Waters of the Senegal River excludes Guinea and Guinea Bissau, the Niger Basin Water Charter excludes Algeria, and the Volta Basin Code of Conduct was contracted by Ghana and Burkina Faso for the Volta River Basin, which is shared by six riparian states (Burkina Faso, Ghana, Benin Republic, Togo, Côte d'Ivoire and Mali).

322 Garane (n 27) at 5.

323 Ibid.

development and improving institutional and legal instruments.[324] Research programs on groundwater under the UNECE Water Convention include the 'Study of the application of the principles of the Convention to transboundary groundwater (2011)', 'Study on groundwater in transboundary water agreements in EECCA (2009)',[325] and physical projects in the UNECE region such as the inventory and assessments of the transboundary rivers, lakes and groundwater carried out consecutively in 2007 and 2011. The results of these studies show the limited attention paid to addressing the consequences of pressures from agriculture, industry, inefficient irrigation and drainage, depletion due to heavy abstraction, pollution due to waste disposal and local mining on the ground water. The Model Provisions on Transboundary Ground waters are non-binding soft law developed under the Convention, and their aim is to guide parties and non-parties when entering into or reviewing bilateral or multilateral agreements on transboundary groundwater, or when considering additional protocol to an existing agreement or a separate specific agreement on groundwater. There are nine model provisions.[326]

In West Africa, as in most other regions, interest in the study of groundwater (confined and unconfined aquifers) is very limited despite the problem

324 Demessin Nurmaganbetov, 'Report of EU Water Initiative National Policy Dialogues on IWRM Core Group meeting: Aral Sea Basin Program—III and synergies with the NPDS/IWRM.' http://www.unece.org/fileadmin/DAM/env/water/npd/Aral_Sea_Basin_Program_%E2%80%93_III_and_synergies_with_the_NPDs_on_IWRM._Demessin_Nurmaganbetov.pdf. (accessed 12 September 2017).

325 The encompassed Eastern Europe, the Caucasus and Central Asia.

326 The UNECE Model Provisions on Transboundary Groundwaters are available on line at https://www.unece.org/fileadmin/DAM/env/water/publications/WAT_model_provisions/ece_mp.wat_40_eng.pdf (accessed 12 September 2016). The Provisions can be summarized as follows: Provision 1: take all appropriate measures to prevent, control and reduce any transboundary impact / use transboundary groundwaters in an equitable and reasonable manner; Provision 2: use transboundary groundwaters in a sustainable manner; Provision 3: cooperate in the common identification, delineation and characterization of transboundary groundwaters/ joint monitoring and assessment of quantity and quality of transboundary groundwaters; Provision 4: integrated management of transboundary groundwaters and surface waters; Provision 5: prevention, control and reduction of the pollution of transboundary groundwaters; Provision 6: exchange of information and available data on transboundary groundwaters; Provision 7: joint or coordinated plans for the proper management of transboundary groundwaters; Provision 8: environmental impact assessments, notification and consultation requirements, access to information and public participation with respect to the conditions of transboundary groundwaters; Provision 9: joint body in order to implement the objectives and principles and coordinate cooperation.

of groundwater over abstraction and depletion. Some transboundary aquifers in West Africa are the Lake Chad Basin Aquifer (Central African Republic, Chad, Cameroon, Niger, and Nigeria), the Liptako-Gourma Aquifer (Burkina Faso and Niger), the Iullemeden Aquifer System (Mali, Niger, and Nigeria), and the Coastal Sedimentary Aquifer System (Ghana, Côte d' Ivoire, Nigeria, Benin, and Togo). None are regulated under a treaty.[327] On the international level, the International Law Commission Draft Articles on the Law of Transboundary Aquifers have yet to be fully adopted by the United Nations General Assembly, and there is no enforceable international instrument for managing the use of transboundary aquifers.[328] However, under the activities of the UNECE Water Convention, the Niger River Basin in West Africa and the North West Sahara Aquifer in North Africa have been selected for a water-food-energy-ecosystems nexus project. The implementation of these groundwater projects, together with the provisions of the Model Provisions on Transboundary Groundwater, have potential value to the study, assessment, management and cooperation on groundwater in West Africa.

In addition to the two projects for groundwater study and assessment under the UNECE Water Convention in Africa, other groundwater projects are implemented in several traansboundary river basins and aquifers under the United Nations Environment Programme/Global Environment Facility (UNEP/GEF) International Waters projects.[329] An example of such a project is the 'Managing Hydrological Risks in the Iullemeden Aquifer,'[330] which reveals that the aquifer is "threatened by aquifer overexploitation, climate change, growing population pressure and human induced water pollution." Other groundwater projects include the 'Mano River Union Ecosystem Conservation and International Water Resources Management (IWRM) Project'[331] and 'Improving IWRM Knowledge-based Management and Governance of the Niger Basin and the Iullemeden_Taoudeni_Tanezrouft Aquifer System (ITTAS).'[332] Other UNEP/GEF projects impacting transboundary surface water and groundwater

327 The Iullemeden Aquifer System is regulated by a limited memorandum of understanding.

328 ILC, Draft Articles on the Law of Transboundary Aquifers, Report of the International Law Commission, Sixtieth Session, UN Doc. A/63/10, Supplement No. 10. http://legal.un.org/ilc/texts/instruments/english/commentaries/8_5_2008.pdf. (accessed 12 September 2017). The Draft Articles have been submitted to the UN General Assembly for adoption.

329 For a description of all International Water projects see http://iwlearn.net (accessed 29 August 2017).

330 See 'Introduction,' *IW:LEARN*, http://iullemeden.iwlearn.org/ (accessed 31 August 2017).

331 The project's objective is conservation of the Upper Guinea forest ecosystem. See http://iwlearn.net/iw-projects/4953 (accessed 15 January 2017).

332 See http://iwlearn.net/iw-projects/5535. (accessed 15 January 2017).

management in West Africa are the 'Accruing Multiple Global Benefits through Integrated Water Resources Management/Water Use Efficiency Planning: A Demonstration Project for Sub-Saharan Africa',[333] 'Addressing Transboundary Concerns in the Volta River Basin and its Downstream Coastal Area'[334] and the Global international Waters Assessment Project (GIWA).[335] Some of the projects are for unpopular transboundary river basins and aquifer systems like the Mano River Basin and the Taoudeni and Tanezrouft Aquifer. As more riparian states in West Africa benefit from environmental projects outside the UNECE, the relevance of the UNECE Water Convention, which is not as popular as the UN Watercourses Convention in the region, will likely diminish. Nevertheless, the UNECE projects could co-exist with the other non-UNECE projects. In the long run, riparian states in West Africa do not need to be a party to the UNECE Water Convention.

4.4 *Climate Change Adaptation Program under the UNECE Water Convention*

Another major achievement of the UNECE Water Convention is the promotion of climate change adaptation and resilience. The UNECE Water Convention recognizes the impact of climate change on transboundary water resources, including its impact on dependent sectors like agriculture and hydropower generation, and has developed programs on climate change adaptation.[336] Major programs in this area include the publication of the 'Guidance on Water and Adaptation to Climate Change'[337] and 'Programs on Adaptation to Climate Change in the Transboundary River Basins' (in cooperation with the International Network of Basin Organizations, the International Union

333 Ibid. The project's objective is to develop knowledge-based management, governance and resources conservation of the Niger Basin and the Iullemeden-Taoudeni/Tanezrouft Aquifer System (ITTAS) and to improve support of IWRM for the benefit of communities and the resilience of ecosystems.

334 See https://www.thegef.org/project/addressing-transboundary-concerns-volta-river-basin-and-its-downstream-coastal-area (accessed 31 August 2017).

335 For additional information on GIWA, see http://www.unep.org/dewa/giwa/ (accessed 15 January 2017).

336 UNECE. "The Water Convention Serving the Planet". *UNECE*. http://www.unece.org/fileadmin/DAM/env/water/publications/brochure/Brochures_Leaflets/A4_trifold_en_web.pdf (accessed 17 January 2017).

337 UNECE, 'Guidance on Water and Adaptation to Climate Change'. (Geneva, United Nations, 2009), http://www.unece.org/fileadmin/DAM/env/water/publications/documents/Guidance_water_climate.pdf. (accessed 26 February 2017).

for Conservation of Nature, the Global Water Partnership and others).[338] Another publication[339] shows where UNECE assists countries in developing transboundary adaptation strategies through guidance, capacity building, groundwater projects, and exchange of experience. Projects on climate change adaptation are conducted on selected river basins and each project is defined by the circumstances of a particular area, for example flood risk management in Eastern Europe (Dniester River Basin and Sava River Basin), IWRM and adaptation in Belarus, Lithuania, and Russia Federation (Neman River Basin), or water scarcity aggravated by the impact of climate change in Central Asia (Chu Talas River Basin). According to Nikiforova, "the projects are focused mainly on developing a joint adaptation strategy through promoting cooperation and exchanging information."[340] The Guidance on Water and Adaptation to Climate Change promotes resilience by providing step-by-step "advice to decision makers and water managers on how to assess impacts of climate change on water quantity and quality, how to perform risk assessment, including health risk assessment, how to gauge vulnerability, and how to design and implement appropriate adaptation strategies."[341]

In the West African, the climate change variability produces extreme drought and increasing water scarcity. In some cases it produces extreme flooding, particularly in regions close to the banks of transboundary watercourses. As a result, West Africa is currently characterized by increased pressure on water and decreased fresh water availability.[342] Both the climate change publications and projects of the UNECE Water Convention could help in addressing the problems associated with managing the impact of climate change on

---

338 Nikiforova (n 315). See Programme of Pilot Projects on Adaptation to Climate Change in Transboundary Basins under the UNECE Water Convention by Sonja Koeppel. http://unfccc.int/files/adaptation/knowledge_resources/databases/partners_action_pledges/application/pdf/unece_furtherinfo2_060511.pdf (accessed 22 September 2017).

339 UNECE. 'How to Adapt Water Management to Climate Change in Transboundary Basins?' *UNECE* 'http://www.unece.org/fileadmin/DAM/env/water/publications/brochure/Brochures_Leaflets/Climate_Change_en_web.pdf. (accessed 17 January 2017).

340 Nikiforova (n 315).

341 UNECE (n 337) at iii.

342 Madiodio Niasse. 'Understanding and Responding to Climate: Induced Water Conflict Risks over Transboundary Watercourses in West Africa'. *in* T. Petermann (ed), *Towards Climate Change Adaptation—Building Adaptive Capacity in Managing African Transboundary River Basins. Case Studies from African Practitioners and Researchers*, pp. 75–88, (Zschortau, Germany, InWEnt, 2008). http://www.orangesenqurak.com/UserFiles/File/Other/InWent_TowardsClimateChangeAdaptation.pdf. (accessed 31 August 2015).

shared water resources, particularly the receding waters of the Lake Chad, extreme drought in the Lake Chad Basin, and part of the Senegal River Basin, and flooding in parts of the Niger River Basin. However, currently the only UNECE project promoting climate change resilience in West Africa is the water-food-energy-ecosystems nexus project in the Niger River Basin.[343]

In West Africa, some river basins have been selected for projects that promote resilience to the impact of climate change under the UNEP/GEF and other organizations. The UNEP/GEF projects include the 'Integrated Development for Increased Rural Climate Resilience in the Niger Basin,'[344] 'Improving Lake Chad Management through Building Climate Change Resilience and Reducing Ecosystem Stress through Implementation of the SAP,'[345] 'Transboundary Diagnostic Analysis of the Lake Chad,' and 'Reversal of Land and Water Degradation Trends in the Lake Chad Basin Ecosystems.' The Lake Chad projects primarily seek to address the problems arising from the shrinking waters of Lake Chad and drought on its ecosystems.[346] Further, the Lake Chad Basin Commission has undertaken a project to transfer water from the Oubangui River Basin in Central Africa to Lake Chad. Another important climate change adaptation project which addressed the vulnerability and impact of climate change in West Africa is the 2004 International Union for Conservation of Nature (IUCN) study in collaboration with Permanent Interstate Committee for Drought Control in the Sahel (CILSS), Global Water Partnership (GWP) and

343 The title of the project is 'Programme for Integrated Development and Climate Change Adaptation in the Niger Basin.' The project aims to improve the resilience of the population through sustainable management of natural resources, agro-pastoral production, silt reduction in the Niger River Basin, resilience of production systems and vulnerable groups enhancement. See UNECE 'Overview of the Activities of the Pilot Projects and Other Basins in the Global Network.' *UNECE* http://www.unece.org/fileadmin/DAM/env/documents/2014/WAT/10Oct_13-15_Geneva/CC_5thworkshop/Overview_pilot_projects_progress_2014.pdf. (accessed 15 January 2015).

344 The project objective is to improve water security, climate resilience, and natural resources management at regional, sub-basin and community levels in the Niger Basin. See http://iwlearn.net/resources/documents/2350 (accessed 15 January 2017).

345 The project objective is to achieve climate resilient, integrated ecosystem-based management of the Lake Chad Basin through implementation of agreed policy, legal and institutional reforms and investments that improve water quality and quantity, protect biodiversity, and sustain livelihoods. See http://iwlearn.net/iw-projects/4748. (accessed 15 January 2017).

346 Some of the Lake Chad Basin projects are implemented by UNEP/GEF in conjunction with the Lake Chad Basin Commission.

Dialogue on Water and Climate.[347] The study revealed a sharp decrease in the rainfall pattern in the Sahel region and the southward movement of the rains which results in severe drought in some areas and flooding in others. The study also recommended four strategies to strengthen "the level of preparedness of the region to tackle the impacts of climate variability and change, in the water sector in particular."[348] The ECOWAS Commission has also adopted some strategies to address climate change vulnerability in West Africa.[349] As earlier recommended for groundwater projects, the UNECE projects on climate change could co-exist with similar projects in West Africa without states becoming contracting parties to the UNECE Water Convention. The UNECE Convention does not offer to West Africa anything more than the UN Watercourses Convention and some of the basin agreements in the region.

Conclusion

As framework conventions, both the UN Watercourses Convention and the UNECE Water Convention have become excellent models for many other

347 Modiodio Naisse et al. (eds.) 'Reducing West Africa Vulnerability to Climate Impact on Water Resources, Wetlands, and Desertification: Elements for a Regional Strategy for Preparedness and Adaptation' http://waterwiki.net/images/1/18/Reducing_West_Africa's_Vulnerability_to_Climate_Impacts_on_Water_Resources,_Wetlands_and_Desertification.pdf (accessed 13 September 2017).

348 The IUCN recommended strategies are "improving and sharing basic scientific knowledge and decision support information; promoting IWRM principles and the ecosystem approach in managing water resources, continental, and coastal wetlands; identifying, promoting, and disseminating appropriate adaptation technologies, techniques, and measures; and setting up a regional consultative framework." The IUCN study notes that creation of the Permanent Interstate Committee for Drought Control in the Sahel (CILSS) is a significant initiative to respond to recurrent drought in the Sahel region of West Africa (ibid.).

349 The ECOWAS strategies are: to strengthen the scientific and technical capacity of the sub-region to reduce vulnerability to climate change; to promote integration of climate change aspects into development at policies, strategies, programs and projects at sub-regional and national levels; and to develop and implement programme and projects on adaptation to climate change at sub regional and national levels. See Bougonou K. DjerI-Alassani, 'Climate Change Concerns Management and Perspectives in ECOWAS Commission, the ECOWAS Change.' https://www.uneca.org/sites/default/files/uploaded-documents/Climate/CCDA1/ccda1_topic4.3_3._presentation_ecowas_commission.pdf (accessed 13 September 2017).

water treaties.[350] Their provisions are applicable for West Africa transboundary water management at the stage of treaty negotiation and implementation. Important provisions of both conventions have the potential to positively influence West African transboundary water resources management in five categories, namely, scope, substantive provisions, procedural provisions, institutional framework and dispute resolution. According to Wouters, the quality of cooperation by watercourse states in any given instrument is determined by the extent to which these elements are adequately addressed in the instrument.[351] Currently, in West Africa, while some water treaties like the Niger Basin Water Charter and Lake Chad Basin Water Charter are greatly influenced by the UN Watercourses Convention, the influence of the UNECE Water Convention is otherwise very limited. Also, while some states in West Africa are contracting parties to the UN Watercourses Convention and more states could join them, no state in West Africa has become a contracting party to the UNECE Water Convention. Instead, some water experts advocate for an "adoption of a regional protocol governing international water systems among the Members of the Economic Community of West African States (ECOWAS), following the example of the Southern Africa Development Community (SADC)."[352]

Before and after negotiating a regional water treaty, states in West Africa do not need to be contracting parties to both the UN Watercourses Convention and the UNECE Water Convention. What West Africa needs is a treaty position that accommodates the reality of the management of its transboundary water resources. Judged by the reluctance of states to become parties to the UN Watercourses Convention, accession by West African states to the UNECE Water Convention might meet similar or worse hurdles. Salman attributes such delays to several factors, including the problem of harmonizing

350 The UNECE Water Convention is the model for the Rhine River and Danube River treaties while the UN Watercourses Convention has influenced provisions of a host of treaties including the Niger Basin Water Charter, SADC Water Protocol, Lake Chad Basin Water Charter and Mekong River Basin Agreement.

351 Patricia Wouters and Huiping Chen 'China's "Soft Path" to Transboundary Water Cooperation Examined in the Light of Two UN Global Water Conventions—Exploring the "Chinese Way"'. *Journal of Water Law*, Vol. 22, No. 6 (2014), pp, 229–47.

352 West Africa: UNWC's Global Relevance,' *UN Watercourses Convention Online User's Guide.* http://www.unwatercoursesconvention.org/global-relevance/west-africa/ (accessed 15 January 2017). The SADC Water Protocol (n 164) was adopted by 11 countries (Republic of South Africa, Lesotho, Tanzania, Malawi, Botswana, Mozambique, Zambia, Zimbabwe, Tanzania, Namibia and Swaziland) to apply to different river basins.

the relationship between the Convention and existing agreements.[353] Further, there is the possible reaction of West African states to a Convention that they might not consider 'their own' and that might be seen as a 'colonialist' tool. A treaty from the region might be more appropriate and acceptable. While the UN Watercourses Convention is considered very adaptable and easy to implement, implementation of the provisions of the UNECE Water Convention requires much more detail and tasks which might be too onerous for West Africa. For example Article 12 of the UNECE Water Convention obliges riparian states to set up and adopt water quality objectives and criteria and to "undertake specific research and development activities in support of achieving and maintaining the water-quality objectives and criteria which they have agreed to set and adopt."[354]

According to Garane, "compliance with the more stringent provisions of the UNECE Water Convention requires significant and foreseeable financial and technical resources, which countries in West Africa now lack."[355] The question for consideration is whether it is worthwhile for states in West Africa to begin to struggle to conform to requirements of a convention that was not initially contracted for the region and which in the long run might hold little benefit to it. The UNECE Water Convention is one of the five UNECE environmental conventions.[356] It was founded on some earlier transboundary water resource policies and declarations of the UNECE.[357] The declarations that later become

353 Salman (n 113).

354 Also under Article 9 of the UNECE Water Convention all riparian states must have joint agreements and institutions that must be adapted to the provisions of the Convention. Article 2(8) provides that riparian states could decide to adopt more stringent provisions than those of the Convention.

355 Garane (n 27) at 27.

356 The other UNECE conventions are the 1979 Convention on Long Range Transboundary Air Pollution, 1991 Convention on Environmental Impact Assessment in a Transboundary Context (Espoo Convention), 1992 Convention on the Transboundry Effects of Industrial Accidents, and the 1999 Convention on Access to Information, Public Participation in Decision Making and Access to Justice in Environmental Matters (Aarhus Convention).

357 The UNECE transboundary water resources declarations that culminated in the UNECE Water Convention are the 1966 ECE Declaration of Policy on Water-pollution Control, the 1980 Declaration of Policy on Prevention and Control of Water Pollution, the 1982 Decision on International Co-operation on Shared Water Resources, the 1984 Declaration of Policy on the Rational Use of Water, the 1986 Decision on Co-operation in the Field of Transboundary Waters, the 1989 Charter on Groundwater Management, and the 1990 Code of Conduct on Accidental Pollution of Transboundary Inland Waters.

the UNECE Water Convention fit the specific need to prevent or mitigate the impact of advanced industrialization in Europe and are not relevant in some regions of Africa.[358] Although the UN formed the United Nations Economic Commission for Africa (UNECA) specifically for Africa, it has not initiated a water treaty for Africa, but it might decide to do so in the future. If this is done, the treaty will be to Africa what the UNECE Water Convention has been to Europe (until its recent amendment to accommodate other regions). Similarly, an ECOWAS water treaty would serve as a multi-basin international water agreement for West Africa.

Though there is a need to address the problems generated by unregulated shared watercourses in West Africa, the important issue is not which global convention the states belong to but how strong and efficient the transboundary water resources management in the region has grown over time. To achieve this goal and to further address major gaps and failings in transboundary water resources management in West Africa, states in the region could negotiate a region-based water treaty to reflect the needs and concerns of the region and supplement it with basin-specific treaties. In West Africa, some norms in the UNECE Water Convention do not provide a suitable regulatory framework for transboundary river basins without instruments or fill the gaps of existing water regimes in the region. Contrarily, states in West Africa could consider becoming a party to the UN Watercourses Convention as it has become the focal point of the principles of customary international water law, is widely endorsed, and is adaptable to any region. According to Salman, the UN Watercourses Convention "is basically a framework convention, which lays down basic principles and procedures, leaving the details to the watercourse states to complement in agreements that take into account the characteristics and uses of their specific watercourse."[359] Hence, adoption of these global treaties by the states of West Africa is not sufficient because "the universal law needs to be complemented by regional or basin agreement."[360] Thus due to the limitation facing adoption of specific basin treaties for every river basin in the region, a regional regime is recommended instead. The UN Watercourses Convention provides the legal framework for negotiating such an agreement because its entry into force gives it the operational visibility that will encourage states to conclude

358 The substantive provisions of the UNECE Water Convention are too detailed and prescriptive regarding water quality standards, precise guidelines and advanced standards of conduct for prevention of transboundary impact. Such advanced standard of conduct as specified in Article 3 of the UNECE Water Convention are 'European' not 'African.'

359 Salman (n 130) at 916.

360 Boisson de Chazournes (n 3) at 10.

agreement in accordance with its principles.[361] Practically, this is how the UN Watercourses Convention which offers benefits globally can fill the gaps and address the failings in water regimes in West Africa as well as provide a regulatory framework for river basins without instruments in place.

Bibliography

Treaties, Soft Law and Statutes

Abuja Declaration on Water: A Key to Sustainable Development in Africa (Final Launch of the African Ministerial Conference on Water (AMCOW)), Abuja, Nigeria, 29–30 April 2002, http://www.africanwater.org/Documents/amcow_declaration.pdf.

Act Regarding Navigation and Economic Co-operation between the States of the Niger Basin, Niamey, 26 October 1963, http://gis.nacse.org/tfdd/tfdddocs/264ENG.pdf.

Agreement between the Federal Republic of Nigeria and the Republic of Niger concerning the Equitable Sharing in the Development, Conservation and Use of their Common Water Resources, 18 August 1990, http://ocid.nacse.org/tfdd/tfdddocs/483ENG.pdf.

Agreement Concerning the Niger River Commission and the Navigation and Transport on the River Niger, Niamey, 25 November 1964, https://iea.uoregon.edu/treaty-text/1964-nigerrivercommissionnavigationtransportrivernigerentxt.

Agreement Governing the Operations of Onchocerciasis Control Program in the Volta River Basin, 1 November 1973, http://www.internationalwaterlaw.org/documents/regionaldocs/1973_Agreement_on_Onchocerciasis_Control_Programme_in_the_Volta_River_Basin_area-English.pdf.

Agreement on the Cooperation for the Sustainable Development of the Mekong River, Chiang Rai, 5 April 1995, http://www.mrcmekong.org/assets/Publications/policies/agreement-Apr95.pdf.

Agreement Revising the Agreement Concerning the Niger River Commission and the Navigation and Transport on the River Niger, Niamey, 15 June 1973, https://iea.uoregon.edu/treaty-text/1973-amendments-1964-nigerrivercommissionnavigationtransportrivernigerentxt.

361 L. Boisson de Chazournes et al. "L'entrée en vigueur de la Convention des Nations Unies sur le droit relatif aux utilisations des cours d'eau internationaux à des fins autres que la navigation (1997)", *Geneva Water Hub*, Note politique no 2 (2015), http://archive-ouverte.unige.ch:80735.

Charter of Waters of the Senegal River, May 2002, http://iea.uoregon.edu/pages/view_treaty.php?t=2002-SenegalRiverWaterCharter.EN.txt&par=view_treaty_html.

Code of Conduct of Sustainable and Equitable Management of Shared Water Resources of the Volta Basin, July 2006, http://www.dialoguebarrages.net/fr/ressources-et-documents/doc_download/122-niger-basin-authority-nba-water-codeConvention.

Statute on Freedom of Transit, Barcelona, 20 April 1921, http://treaties.fco.gov.uk/docs/fullnames/pdf/1923/TS0027%20(1923)%20CMD-1992%201921%2020%20APR,%20BARCELONA%3B%20CONVENTION%20&%20STATUTE%20ON%20FREEDOM%20OF%20TRANSIT.pdf.

Convention and Statute Relating to the Development of the Lake Chad Basin, Fort Lamy, 22 May 1964, https://iea.uoregon.edu/treaty-text/1964-developmentchadbasinconventionentxt.

Convention Concerning the Status of the Senegal River, Nouakchott, 11 March 1972, https://iea.uoregon.edu/treaty-text/1972-senegalriverstatusfrtxt.

Convention Concluded between Mali, Mauritania and Senegal Regarding the Legal Status of Common Works, Bamako, 21 December 1978, https://iea.uoregon.edu/treaty-text/1978-statutouvragescommunsfrtxt.

Convention Creating the Niger Basin Authority, Faranah, 21 November 1980, http://iea.uoregon.edu/pages/view_treaty.php?t=1980-NigerBasinAuthority.EN.txt&par=view_treaty_html.

Convention on Biological Diversity, Rio de Janeiro, 5 June 1992, https://www.cbd.int/doc/legal/cbd-en.pdf.

Convention on Co-operation for the Protection and Sustainable Use of the Danube River, Sofia, 29 June 1994, http://faolex.fao.org/docs/pdf/mul17444.pdf.

Convention on Environmental Impact Assessment in a Transboundary Context, Espoo, 25 February 1991, http://www.unece.org/env/eia/about/eia_text.html.

Convention on Revision of the General Act of Berlin and General Acts and Declaration of Brussels, Saint-Germain-en-Laye, 10 September 1919, https://www.loc.gov/law/help/us-treaties/bevans/m-ust000002-0261.pdf.

Convention on the Law of Non-navigational Uses of International Watercourses, New York, 21 May 1997, http://legal.un.org/ilc/texts/instruments/english/conventions/8_3_1997.pdf.

Convention on the Law of the Sea, Montego Bay, 10 December 1982, http://www.un.org/depts/los/convention_agreements/texts/unclos/unclos_e.pdf.

Convention on the Law of Treaties, Vienna, 30 November 1969, http://www.oas.org/legal/english/docs/Vienna%20Convention%20Treaties.htm.

Convention on the Protection and the Use of Transboundary Watercourses and International Lakes, Helsinki, 17 March 1992, http://www.unece.org/fileadmin/DAM/env/water/pdf/watercon.pdf.

Convention on the Protection of the Rhine, Rotterdam, 22 January 1998, http://www.internationalwaterlaw.org/documents/regionaldocs/rhine_river.html.

Convention on the Status of the Volta River and Establishment of Volta Basin Authority, http://iea.uoregon.edu/pages/view_treaty.php?t=2007-VoltaBasinAuthority.EN.txt&par=view_treaty_html.

Convention Pertaining to the Creation of the Organization for the Management of the Senegal River, Nouakchott, 11 March 1972, https://iea.uoregon.edu/base-agreement-list/Senegal%20River%20Basin.

Convention Regarding the Methods of Financing Joint Works, Bamako, 12 May 1982, https://iea.uoregon.edu/treaty-text/1982-senegalriverfinancingmodalitiescommonworksfrtxt.

Convention Relating to Creation of Gambia River Basin Development Organisation, Kaolack, 30 June 1978, http://www.fao.org/docrep/w7414b/w7414b0c.htm.

Convention Relating to the General Development of the Senegal River, Bamakoon, 26 July 1963, https://iea.uoregon.edu/treaty-text/1963-bamakosenegalriverbasinfrtxt.

Convention Relating to the Status of the River Gambia, Kaolack, 30 June 1978, http://www.fao.org/docrep/w7414b/w7414b0b.htm#TopOfPage.

Declaration of the United Nations Conference on the Human Environment, Stockholm, 5–16 June 1972, http://www.unep.org/Documents.Multilingual/Default.asp?documentid=97&articleid=1503.

Declaration on Environment and Development, Rio de Janeiro, 3–14 June 1992, http://www.un.org/documents/ga/conf151/aconf15126-1annex1.htm.

Economic Community of West African States, West Africa Water Resources Policy, 19 December 2008, http://cmsdata.iucn.org/downloads/wawrp.pdf.

European Union, Directive 2000/60/EC of the European Parliament and of the Council of 23 October 2000 establishing a framework for Community action in the field of water policy, http://ec.europa.eu/environment/water/water-framework/index_en.html.

General Act of the Conference of Berlin, Berlin, 26 February 1885, http://waado.org/colonial_rule/general_documents/berlin_act_1885.html.

Helsinki Rules on the Uses of the Waters of International Rivers, Helsiniki, August 1966, http://www.colsan.edu.mx/investigacion/aguaysociedad/proyectofrontera/helsinki%20rules%201966.pdf.

International Law Commission (ILC), Draft Articles on Prevention of Transboundary Harm from Hazardous Activities, Report of the International Law Commission, Fifty-third Session, UN Doc. A/56/10, Supplement No. 10, http://legal.un.org/ilc/texts/instruments/english/commentaries/9_7_2001.pdf.

ILC, Draft Articles on the Law of Transboundary Aquifers, Report of the International Law Commission, Sixtieth Session, UN Doc. A/63/10, Supplement No. 10, http://legal.un.org/ilc/texts/instruments/english/commentaries/8_5_2008.pdf.

Niger Basin Water Charter, Niamey, 30 April 2008, https://iea.uoregon.edu/treaty-text/2008-nigerbasinwatercharterfrtxt.

Protocol of the Agreement between Republic of Guinea and Republic of Guinea Bissau on the Management of River Koliba-Korubal, Conakry, 21 October, 1978, http://gis.nacse.org/tfdd/tfdddocs/403FRE.pdf.

Revised Convention Pertaining to Creating the Niger Basin Authority, N'Djamena, 29 October 1987, http://ocid.nacse.org/tfdd/tfdddocs/468FRE.pdf.

Revised Protocol on Shared Watercourses in the Southern African Development Community, Windhoek, 7 August 2000, http://www.internationalwaterlaw.org/documents/regionaldocs/Revised-SADC-SharedWatercourse-Protocol-2000.pdf.

United Nations Committee on Economic, Social and Cultural Rights, General Comment No. 15—The Right to Water (Articles 11 and 12 of the International Covenant on Economic, Social and Cultural Rights, Committee on Economic, Social and Cultural Rights), 20 January 2003, UN Doc. E/C.12/2002/11, http://www.refworld.org/docid/4538838d11.html.

United Nations Conference on Environment and Development, Agenda 21, Rio de Janerio, 3–14 June 1992, https://sustainabledevelopment.un.org/content/documents/Agenda21.pdf.

United Nations Economic Commission for Europe (UNECE), Convention on Access to Information, Public Participation in Decision-Making and Access to Justice in Environmental Matters, Aarhus, 25 June 1998, http://www.unece.org/fileadmin/DAM/env/pp/documents/cep43e.pdf.

UNECE, Model Provisions on Transboundary Groundwaters, New York and Geneva, 2014, https://www.unece.org/fileadmin/DAM/env/water/publications/WAT_model_provisions/ece_mp.wat_40_eng.pdf.

UNECE, Protocol on Civil Liability, http://www.unece.org/fileadmin/DAM/env/civil-liability/documents/protocol_e.pdf.

UNECE, Protocol on Water and Health, http://www.unece.org/fileadmin/DAM/env/documents/2000/wat/mp.wat.2000.1.e.pdf.

United Nations General Assembly, The Human Right to Water and Sanitation, UN Doc. A/Res64/292, 28 July 2010.

Water Charter for the Lake Chad Basin, 13 April 2012, https://www.africanwaterfacility.org/fileadmin/uploads/awf/Projects/MULTIN-LAKECHAD-Water-Charter.pdf.

Water Resources Act (Nigeria) Cap W2 LFN 2004.

Books, Journals and Internet Sources

Abseno, M. M., "The Influence of the UN Watercourses Convention on the Development of a treaty Regime in the Nile River Basin," *Water International*, Vol. 38, No. 3 (March 2013), pp. 192–203.

African Ministers' Council on Water http://www.amcow-online.org/index.php?option=com_content&view=article&id=115&Itemid=71&lang=en.

Atlas on Regional Integration in West Africa: Transboundary River Basins,' ECOWAS-SWAC and Organisation for Economic Cooperation and Development (2006), http://www.oecd.org/swac/publications/38409569.pdf.

Ayibotele, N. B., 'Senegal—Establishing a Transboundary Organisation for IWRM in the Senegal River Basin Case #45,' (n.d.), https://brucehooper.files.wordpress.com/2016/10/transboundary-establishing-a-transboundary-organisation-for-iwrm-in-the-senegal-river-basin-45.pdf.

Beach, H. L. et al., *Transboundary Freshwater Dispute Resolution* (New York, United Nations University Press, 2000).

Boisson de Chazournes, L., M. Tignino, & K. Sangbana, "L'entrée en vigueur de la Convention des Nations Unies sur le droit relatif aux utilisations des cours d'eau internationaux à des fins autres que la navigation (1997)", Geneva Water Hub, Note politique no 2 (2015), https://www.genevawaterhub.org/sites/default/files/atoms/files/2015.02.17.pb_fr_convention1997_lbc_mt_ks.pdf.

Boisson de Chazournes, L., "Freshwater and International Law: the Interplay between Universal, Regional and Basin Perspectives". Available online at http://archive-ouverte.unige.ch:5080.

Chayes, A., & A. H. Chayes, 'On Compliance,' *International Organization*, Vol. 47, No. 2 (Spring 1993), pp. 175–205.

Demessin, N., Demessin Nurmaganbetov, 'Report of EU Water Initiative National Policy Dialogues on IWRM Core Group meeting: Aral Sea Basin Program—III and synergies with the NPDS/IWRM,' http://www.unece.org/fileadmin/DAM/env/water/npd/Aral_Sea_Basin_Program_%E2%80%93_III_and_synergies_with_the_NPDs_on_IWRM._Demessin_Nurmaganbetov.pdf.

Djeri-Alassani, B. K. 'Climate Change Concerns Management and Perspectives in ECOWAS Commission, the ECOWAS Change.' https://www.uneca.org/sites/default/files/uploaded-documents/Climate/CCDA1/ccda1_topic4.3_3._presentation_ecowas_commission.pdf.

ECOWAS, 'Basic Information,' http://www.ecowas.int/about-ecowas/basic-information.

Garane, A. 'UN Watercourses Convention: Applicability and Relevance in West Africa,' (Global Water Partnership, WWF, Green Cross and UNESCO Centre of Water Law, Policy and Science, 2008), http://internationalwaterlaw.org/bibliography/WWF/RA_West_Africa.pdf.

Garretson, A. H., et al. (eds), *The Law of International Drainage Basins* (New York, Oceana Publications, 1967).

Grogan, D., 'Transboundary Water Governance in the Volta River Basin,' *Tufts Wikis* (4 April 2010), https://wikis.uit.tufts.edu/confluence/display/aquapedia/Transboundary+Water+Governance+in+the+Volta+River+Basin.

'Joint Management of Transboundary Water Resources: The OMVG Experience,' *Gambia River Basin Development Organisation*, http://strategicforesight.com/conference_pdf/Presentation%20by%20OMVG.pdf.

Kinna, R., et al., 'Global UN Water Conventions: Options for Coordinated Implementation,' http://www.unwatercoursesconvention.org/documents/discussion-paper-global-un-water-conventions-options-for-coordinated-implementation.pdf.

Koeppel, S., 'Programme of Pilot Projects on Adaptation to Climate Change in Transboundary Basins under the UNECE Water Convention' http://unfccc.int/files/adaptation/knowledge_resources/databases/partners_action_pledges/application/pdf/unece_furtherinfo2_060511.pdf.

Leb, C., *Cooperation in the Law of Transboundary Water Resources* (Cambridge, Cambridge University Press, 2013).

Loures, F., & A. Rieu-Clarke (eds), *The UN Watercourses Convention in Force: Strengthening International Law for Transboundary Water Management* (London & New York, Routledge, 2013).

Mbengue, M., 'A Model for African Shared Water Resources: the Senegal River Legal System.' *Review of European Community and International Environmental Law*, Vol. 23, No. 1 (2014), pp. 59–66.

McCaffrey, S. C., 'Convention on the Law of Non-navigational Uses of International Watercourses,' *United Nations Audiovisual Library of International Law*, http://legal.un.org/avl/ha/clnuiw/clnuiw.html.

McCaffrey, S. C., *The Law of International Watercourses* (2nd edition, Oxford, Oxford University Press, 2007).

McIntyre, O., 'The Role of Customary Rules and Principles of International Environmental Law in the Protection of Shared International Freshwater Resources,' Natural Resources Journal, Vol 46 (2006), pp. 157–210, http://lawschool.unm.edu/nrj/volumes/46/1/06_mcintyre_customary.pdf.

McIntyre, O., 'Utilisation (and Environmental Protection) of Shared International Freshwaters: The Role (and Meaning) of "Equity",' Presentation at the 5th Annual International Water Law and Transboundary Freshwaters Workshop, Dundee, 9–13 June 2014.

McIntyre, O., 'Utilization of Shared International Freshwater Resources: The Meaning and Role of "Equity" in International Water Law,' *Water International*, Vol. 38, No. 2 (2013), pp. 112–29.

Mostert, E., *Conflict and Co-operation in the Management of International Freshwater Resources: A Global Review*, PCCP Series No. 19 (Paris, UNESCO, 2003), http://unesdoc.unesco.org/images/0013/001333/133305e.pdf.

Niasse, M., 'Understanding and Responding to Climate Induced Water Conflict Risks over Transboundary Watercourses in West Africa,' *in* T. Petermann (ed), *Towards Climate Change Adaptation—Building Adaptive Capacity in Managing African*

Transboundary River Basins. Case Studies from African Practitioners and Researchers, pp. 75–88, (Zschortau, Germany, InWEnt, 2008), http://www.orangesenqurak.com/UserFiles/File/Other/InWent_TowardsClimateChangeAdaptation.pdf.

Naisse, M. et al. (eds), 'Reducing West Africa Vulnerability to Climate Impact on Water Resources, Wetlands, and Desertification: Elements for a Regional Strategy for Preparedness and Adaptation' http://waterwiki.net/images/1/18/Reducing_West_Africa's_Vulnerability_to_Climate_Impacts_on_Water_Resources,_Wetlands_and_Desertification.pdf.

Nikiforova, N., 'International Conventions on Transboundary Waters: Global Solution to Regional Challenges,' Presentation at the 1st International Conference on Energy and Water, Luanda, 25–27 September 2013, http://www.aceew.org/apresentacoes/26/7.pdf?PHPSESSID=62uihl96ajftdm57plkd5q07e2.

Nikiforova, N., '20 years' Experience in Implementing the UNECE Water Convention,' Presentation at the 5th Annual International Water Law and Transboundary Freshwaters Workshop, Dundee, 9–13 June 2014.

Ochoa, C., 'Corporate Social Responsibility and Firm Compliance: Lessons from the International Law-International Relations Discourse,' *Santa Clara Journal of International Law*, Vol. 9 (2011), 169–78.

Odili, N. C., *The Relevance and Application of the 1997 United Nations Watercourses Convention and the 1992 UNECE Water Convention to Transboundary Water Resources Management in West Africa*, (LL.M.thesis, University of Dundee, March 2015).

Rieu-Clarke, A., 'Transboundary Water Sharing and Conflict: A Review of Best Practices,' (Centre for Water Law, Policy and Science, University of Dundee, 2009).

Rieu-Clarke, A., & R. Kinna, 'Can Two Global UN Water Conventions Effectively Co-exist? Making the Case for a "Package Approach" to Support Institutional Coordination,' *Review of European, Comparative & International Environmental Law*, Vol. 23, No. 1 (April 2014), pp. 15–31.

Rieu-Clarke, A., P. Wouters, & F. Loures, 'The Role and Relevance of the UN Convention on the Non-navigational Uses of International Watercourses to the EU and its Member States,' *Centre for Water Law, Policy and Science, University of Dundee*, n.d., http://internationalwaterlaw.org/bibliography/WWF/RA_European_Union.pdf.

Rieu-Clarke, A., et al., *UN Watercourses Convention: User's Guide* (IHP-HELP, Centre for Water Law, Policy and Science, University of Dundee, 2012).

Romanin Jacur, F., A. Bonfanti & S. Francesco (eds), *Natural Resources Grabbing: An International Law Perspective* (Leiden, Brill Nijhoff, 2015).

Salman, M. A. S., 'Niger River,' *Max Planck Encyclopedia of Public International Law*, http://opil.ouplaw.com/view/10.1093/law:epil/9780199231690/law-9780199231690-e1325?prd=EPIL.

Salman, M. A. S., 'The Future of International Water Law: Regional Approaches to Shared Watercourses?,' *in* M. H. Arsanjani, J. K. Cogan, R. D. Sloane and S. Wiessner (eds), *Looking to the Future: Essays on International Law in Honor of W. Michael Reisman*, pp. 907–28 (The Hague, Martinus Nijhoff Publishers, (2011), http://www.internationalwaterlaw.org/experts/Salman.pdf.

Salman M. A. S., 'The United Nations Watercourses Convention Ten Years Later—Why Has its Entry into Force Proven Difficult?,' *Water International*, Vol. 32, No. 1 (2007), pp. 1–15, http://www.unwatercoursesconvention.org/images/2012/10/Salman-UNWatercoursesConventionTenYears.pdf.

Sangbana, K. "La Gestion Intégrée des Ressources en eaux Partagées et les Organismes de Bassin en Afrique: Les cas de l'Autorité du Bassin du Niger et de l'Autorité du Bassin de la Volta", *in* Société Français pour le Droit International, *L'eau en droit International, Colloque de Orléans*–(Paris, A. Pedone, 2011).

'Senegal River Basin,' *International Waters Governance*, http://www.internationalwatersgovernance.com/senegal-river-basin.html.

'Soft Law and Legal Definition,' *USLegal*, http://definitions.uslegal.com/s/soft-law/.

'Streamflow Protection,' *State of Vermont, Agency of Natural Resources, Department of Environmental Conservation, Watershed Management Division*, http://www.vtwaterquality.org/rivers/htm/rv_flowprotection.htm.

Subedi, S., *International Watercourse Law for 21st Century: The Case of River Ganges Basin* (Hampshire, Ashgate, 2005).

Tabarly, S., "La frontière, discontinuités et dynamiques: Bassins versants transfrontaliers en Afrique occidentale", *Geoconfluences, DGESCO—ENS de Lyon* (2008), 'http://geoconfluences.ens-lyon.fr/doc/typespace/frontier/FrontDoc.htm.

Tanzi, A., & M. Arcari, *The United Nations Convention on the Law of International Watercourses: A Framework for Sharing* (London, Kluwer Law International, 2001).

Tanzi, A., 'The Relationship between the 1992 UNECE Convention on the Protection and Use of Transboundary Watercourses and International Lakes and the 1997 UN Convention on the Law of the Non Navigational Uses of International Watercourses, Report of the UNECE Task Force on Legal and Administrative Aspects,' *UNECE* (Geneva, February 2000), http://www.unece.org/fileadmin/DAM/env/water/publications/documents/conventiontotal.pdf.

'The United Nations Convention on the Law of the Non-Navigational Uses of International Watercourses and West Africa Transboundary Water Systems,' (ECOWAS, Global Water Partnership, Green Cross, International Water Association, WWF, and UNESCO Centre for Water Law, Policy and Science, April 2011).

Tignino, M., & K. Sangbana," Le statut d'ouvrages communs et le partages des bénéfices dans les bassins du fleuve Sénégal et Niger", *Geneva Water Hub* (2016), pp. 1–7, https://archive-ouverte.unige.ch/unige:80736.

Tignino, M., & K. Sagbana (eds), *Public Participation and Water Resources Management: Where Do We Stand in International Law?* (Paris, UNESCO, 2015).

'United Nations Economic Commission for Africa,' Green Growth Knowledge Platform, http://www.greengrowthknowledge.org/organization/united-nations-economic-commission-africa-uneca.

United Nations, 'UN Watercourses Convention and the UNECE Water Convention,' UN Watercourses Convention User's Guide Fact Sheet Series No. 12, http://www.unwatercoursesconvention.org/documents/UNWC-Fact-Sheet-12-Relationship-with-UNECE-Water-Convention.pdf.

United Nations, 'Water Resources, A Reason for Cooperation Not Conflict,' *United Nations News Centre* (22 November 2016), http://www.un.org/apps/news/story.asp?NewsID=55626#.WFFeUrIrLIU.

United Nations Economic Commission for Europe (UNECE), 'Guidance on Water and Adaptation to Climate Change,' (Geneva, United Nations, 2009) http://www.unece.org/fileadmin/DAM/env/water/publications/documents/Guidance_water_climate.pdf.

UNECE, 'The Water Convention: Serving the Planet,' *UNECE*, http://www.unece.org/fileadmin/DAM/env/water/publications/brochure/Brochures_Leaflets/A4_trifold_en_web.pdf.

UNECE, 'How to Adapt Water Management to Climate Change in Transboundary Basins?,' *UNECE*, http://www.unece.org/fileadmin/DAM/env/water/publications/brochure/Brochures_Leaflets/Climate_Change_en_web.pdf. UNECE, 'Overview of the Activities of the Pilot Projects and Other Basins in the Global Network,' UNECE, http://www.unece.org/fileadmin/DAM/env/documents/2014/WAT/10Oct_13-15_Geneva/CC_5thworkshop/Overview_pilot_projects_progress_2014.pdf.

UNECE, *Guide to Implementing the Water Convention* (New York and Geneva, United Nations, 2013).

UNECE, *River Basin Commissions and Other Institutions for Transboundary Water Cooperation* (New York and Geneva, United Nations, 2009).

United Nations Environment Programme (UNEP), 'Atlas of International Freshwater Agreements,' (Nairobi, UNEP, 2002), http://www.transboundarywaters.orst.edu/publications/atlas/.

UN Watercourses Convention online Users' Guide, 'The Relationship with the UNECE Convention' http://www.unwatercoursesconvention.org/importance/the-relationship-with-the-unece-water-convention/.

Vinogradov, S. et al., *Transforming Potential Conflict into Cooperation Potential: The Role of International Water Law*, PCCP Series No. 2 (Paris, UNESCO, 2003).

'West Africa: UNWC's Global Relevance,' UN Watercourses Convention Online User's Guide, http://www.unwatercoursesconvention.org/global-relevance/west-africa/.

Wouters, P., & H. Chen, 'China's "Soft Path" to Transboundary Water Cooperation examined in the light of Two UN Global Water Conventions—Exploring the "Chinese Way",' *Journal of Water Law*, Vol. 22, No. 6 (2014), pp, 229–47.

Wouters, P., & S. Vinogradov, 'Analysing the ECE Water Convention: What Lessons for the Regional Management of Transboundary Water Resources?,' *Yearbook of International Co-operation on Environment and Development* (2003/04), pp. 55–63.

Wouters, P., 'The Legal Response to International Water Scarcity and Water Conflicts: The UN Watercourses Convention and Beyond,' *The Water Page*, http://www.africanwater.org/pat_wouters1.htm.

Yongxuan, G., & A. Margolies, 'Transboundary Water Governance in the Volta River Basin,' *Tufts Wikis*, https://wikis.uit.tufts.edu/confluence/display/aquapedia/Transboundary+Water+Governance+in+the+Volta+River+Basin.

www.ingramcontent.com/pod-product-compliance
Lightning Source LLC
Chambersburg PA
CBHW071354230926
51846CB00002B/554
9789004364820